RAVE REVIEWS FOR eMILLIONS

"**Y**ou learn from the success and failure of others. Tang's selection of some of the most influential stars in the Internet world and their inspirational stories make for some very valuable information. This book is a must-have on every Internet marketer's bookshelf."

Joseph Sugarman
Chairman, BluBlocker Corporation,
and Best-Selling Author of *Triggers*

"**S**tanley Tang breaks-open the code on how the moguls really got their starts and created their breaks. eMillions reveals how the pillars of Internet Marketing built their foundations and the lessons these gurus hold critical for you and I to know.

Learn seminal facts about Internet Marketing: When Mark Joyner wrote the very first e-book, why Tom Beal and Gary Ambrose give entrepreneurial credit to the North American Filsaime Butterfly and how Michel Fortin set the first million-dollar-day record.

Stanley got the real players to reveal what they did right and what they would do differently. This is a brave book worth serious consideration to every Internet Marketer."

Ben Mack
#1 Best-Selling Author of *Think Two Products Ahead*
www.ThinkTwoProductsAhead.com

"Inspiring. Intriguing. Informative.

Stanley Tang has pulled together a star-studded cast, and then with penetrating questions, gets them to spill the secrets of their massive success. Every aspiring Internet entrepreneur will find value and motivation in the lessons these pioneers teach in the 14 interviews."

Dr. Mani Sivasubramanian
Infopreneur and Heart Surgeon
www.MoneyPowerWisdom.com

"*eMillions* is exactly the kind of book we need right now – real people making significant inroads to online success. I am honored to be interviewed with these intelligent, successful, entrepreneurs. *eMillions* is an essential reading for the online entrepreneur."

Robin Cowie
Producer of *The Blair Witch Project*,
and President, Worldwide Brands Inc.
www.WorldwideBrands.com

"Stealing some of the insights and advice from those who have been there and done that is one of the very best things you can do to balloon your income online. In fact, Tony Robbins preaches about finding someone who is highly successful and modeling after them.

In *eMillions*, Stanley has provides just that – the real 'in the trenches' insights – behind millions of dollars worth of pure 'real life' results from some of the brightest minds around. I fully recommend you stop what you are doing and go through this. If you are not excited or driven after going through *eMillions*, you'll need to check your pulse."

Eric Louviere
Online Copywriter and Marketer
www.JobCrusher.com

"*eMillions* is a fantastic walk through the brains of some of the best business builders online. I believe strongly in learning from other people's successes and mistakes – especially their mistakes, as it's a lot cheaper when somebody else has already made the mistake and you can avoid it.

Stanley has deftly drawn out the ups and downs, and each story is worthy of some serious study – if you're serious about being successful yourself. I recommend reading only one marketer's story each night, and fully focusing on what they did right and what they did wrong.

As you read through their stories, you'll find that they are regular human beings just like you, and you'll realize how you too can have this success. They've already gone there; you can use ideas from their stories to make your path there that much easier."

Kevin Riley
Osaka, Japan
www.ProductCreationLabs.com

"Stanley did an amazing job pulling together some of the top names in the Internet marketing arena and getting them to spill their guys on exactly how they became successful. I like how in the interviews Stanley goes from square one discussing life first and then transitioning into business. So there are not only inspiring life stories, there are great business lessons as well. *eMillions* is a fantastic read for the new as well as seasoned marketer.

Jason James
Internet Millionaire
www.TheRealIM.com

"**F**acts tell and stories sell. Well, I'm sold! Stanley, I don't know how you got the top notch marketers you did to share their intimate success stories... but you did, and I thank you. It's one thing to just read content, but to be able to go behind the scenes and see that they are REAL people from humble beginnings (even welfare, bankruptcy, and horrific tragedies) who fought their way to the top is priceless. My perspective and attitude has changed and, as a result, my business will never be the same. With no excuse, no obstacle too big, and this book in hand, there's nothing left but to succeed."

Jason Stanley Marshall
Next Internet Millionaire Contestant
www.JasonStanleyMarshall.com

"**I**f I had to sum this book up in two words, they'd be: Absolutely incredible.

Reading about the success stories of some of the biggest names in Internet marketing sent shivers down my spine. And learning the intimate details about how they got to be where they are, how they think and how they run things is motivation enough for anyone to get started.

After reading this book, you'll want to jump up and get started. It's a true inspiration to anyone in this business. I don't read too many books on Internet marketing anymore, but this is one I'll read again and again."

Justin Michie
Author of *Street Smart Internet Marketing*
www.InternetMarketingBook.com

"**I**f you are struggling to get started online or you want to go to the next level, you MUST read *eMillions*."

Reed Floren
Well-Known Joint Venture Broker
www.TheJVBroker.com

**BEHIND-THE-SCENES STORIES OF
14 SUCCESSFUL INTERNET MILLIONAIRES**

STANLEY TANG

madeeasy

AN IMPRINT OF MORGAN JAMES PUBLISHING LLC, NEW YORK

eMillions

By Stanley Tang

© 2008 All rights reserved.

No part of this publication may be reproduced or transmitted in any form or by any means, mechanical or electronic, including photocopying and recording, or by any information storage and retrieval system, without permission in writing from author or publisher (except by a reviewer, who may quote brief passages and/or show brief video clips in a review).

ISBN: 978-1-93359-619-8 (Paperback)
Library of Congress Control Number: 2008931093

Disclaimer

Published by:

AN IMPRINT OF MORGAN JAMES PUBLISHING

Morgan James Publishing, LLC
1225 Franklin Ave. Suite 325
Garden City, NY 11530-1693
800.485.4943
www.MorganJamesPublishing.com

Peninsula
Building Partner

Cover & Interior Designs by:

Megan Johnson
Johnson2Design
www.Johnson2Design.com
megan@Johnson2Design.com

ACKNOWLEDGEMENTS

eMillions has been a very special project for me and I owe thanks to many people for helping me with my first book. First and foremost, I want to acknowledge the sacrifice and effort my father and mother made during the long hours of creating this book; to my sister for her care and encouragement. I love you all.

I want to express my gratitude to the co-authors that made up the *eMillions* team: Mark Joyner, Gary Ambrose, Tom Beal, Joel Christopher, Rob Cowie, Willie Crawford, Michel Fortin, Andrew Fox, Rosalind Gardner, Jermaine Griggs, Jason James, Stu Mclaren and Jeremy Schoemaker. Without all your contributions, this book would have never been created in the first place and my dream of bringing this book to the world would have never been realized.

I am also deeply grateful to the amazing people at Morgan James Publishing for giving me this opportunity to transform my vision into reality. To my mentor, Warren Whitlock, for his book marketing expertise and guidance. To my editor, Virginia Anne Unkefer, for her editorial advice and the ability to make my book worthy of publishing. To Reed Floren, Eric Louviere, Ben Mack, Dr. Mani, Jason Marshall, Justin Michie, Kevin Riley and Joe Sugarman for taking the time to look over my manuscript and giving me helpful comments. To Mike Filsaime, Seth Godin, Robert Kiyosaki, John Reese and Donald Trump for their inspirational teachings. To my Business Studies teacher Mr. Richard St. Paul for his encouragement. To my loyal friends for their spirit and support: Yuvraj, Victor, Jayant, Michael, Daryl, Rushit, Fergus.

And lastly, but most importantly, to my loyal subscribers and customers! Thank to all of you.

TABLE OF CONTENTS

CHAPTER 1
Mark Joyner: The Godfather of Internet Marketing

How a Former U.S. Army Officer Turned a Fledgling One-Man Operation into a Multi-Million Dollar International Corporation with Customers in Every Internet-Connected Country on the Planet

CHAPTER 2
Jermaine Griggs: Founder of HearandPlay.com

How a 17 Year-Old Inner-City Kid with $70 Built a $3 Million Dollar Internet Company from the Ground Up by Teaching People How to Play Piano by Ear

CHAPTER 3
Tom Beal: VP of Operations for MikeFilsaime.com

The Incredible Human Being who Overcame Adversity, Survived Death, and Went On to Become a Successful Internet Entrepreneur

CHAPTER 13
Jeremy Schoemaker: Founder of ShoeMoney Media Group

How an "Average Joe" From Nebraska Went From Zero to $12 Million Dollars in Five Short Years

CHAPTER 14
Andrew Fox: Internet Super Affiliate

How a 26 Year-Old Kid – Who Used To Wash Cars for $5 Per Hour – Generates Instant $70,697, $29,013 and $90,389 Commission Profit Pay Days

FOREWORD

FOREWORD

This book illustrates for us a new phenomenon – well, two actually.

OK, make that three.

First, it demonstrates how prosperity is easily within the grasp of anyone who dares grab it.

The entrepreneurs Stanley has interviewed are one and all "self made" people who started with nothing and shot to stardom.

Well – shot *themselves* to stardom is a more accurate way of putting it.

Next, it illustrates just how easy it is to create valuable information products. All Stanley had to do to put this book together was interview a series of experts and – poof! – he has a sellable product on his hands.

This is but one of the many fast ways to turn information into money – many others are illustrated in this book itself.

Finally, this book illustrates how meritocracy is now at hand.

Throughout history attaining wealth was more or less difficult for the "average guy." Until recent years, however, most of the wealth accumulated throughout history has been done so by people who were granted that right through birth – by class, caste, or so-called "divine right."

With the advent of the internet, more and more we see wealth being granted to people based solely on *merit*.

I for one have no special birth-rights. I was born into as miserable a situation as one could imagine in the United States, but here I am. Google "Mark Joyner" and you can see what I've been able to accomplish. If I had been born into a different era, I can't imagine success would have come so easily for me.

Not that it was easy, but relative to how difficult it would have been had I been born into Mao's Cultural Revolution or the Dark Ages – well, pretty damn easy.

As it will be for you, too.

And to put this into full perspective – and to let you know just how deep this meritocracy runs – you should know this one fact:

When Stanley Tang put this book together he was 15 years old.

Now…

What will you, dear reader, do with the era into which you've been born?

Mark Joyner
Auckland, New Zealand
http://www.markjoyner.name

INTRODUCTION

You've heard about all the wealth being made online. You've heard about the Internet marketers who are silently making millions of dollars... while you sleep, while you work... all the time!

With online sales projected to hit $204 billion in 2008, it's no surprise that the Internet has created more millionaires than any other industry in the history of mankind.

You see it in the news all the time: Some college dropout comes out of nowhere and makes headline news when his website gets bought out for millions of dollars. An overnight millionaire? A lucky get-rich-quick scheme that pulled off?

Wrong.

Nothing could be further from the truth. Indeed, stories like this do create the illusion of instant success. But, when you look behind-the-scenes of those breakthrough successes, what you find are actually motivating stories of individuals who made it happen. The years of hard work, sweat and toil behind a closed door; the build-ups before the breakthroughs. They had a vision, took a path, and persevered against monumental odds.

None of them were overnight successes.

A burning desire consumed me. I began on a mission to extract the real-life success stories from the greatest Internet millionaires of our time, and share their stories and success secrets with the world.

I searched the Internet for months and months to find someone who could help me. Then, as if by magic, one-by-one, the world's top Internet entrepreneurs started crossing my path.

1

I wanted to find out exactly how they overcame adversity to achieve success. I wanted to know everything – the highs, the lows, the trials, the failures. So to cut straight to the chase and get down to the nitty-gritty...

I asked them.

Yes, I interviewed them over the phone and drilled them right down to the bones! I asked every question I could think of. I got the gurus to reveal everything they had down their sleeves. Nothing was held back.

Eight months later, *eMillions* was born.

In this book, 14 of the world's most successful Internet marketers share their inspirational stories, as they walk through their personal lives and the never-before-revealed journey they took to become Internet millionaires! You'll become privy to their struggles, their successes, their biggest mistakes, their mindsets, and their motivations.

As Tony Robbins once said,

"If you want to be successful, find someone who has achieved the results you want and copy what they do and you'll achieve the same results."

— TONY ROBBINS, THE WORLD'S #1 PEAK
PERFORMANCE COACH

I want to make sure you have access to those real-life success stories that you can model your business after. You'll know exactly what works and what doesn't, helping you avoid years of guesswork and frustration.

But let me make one thing perfectly clear:

These are not the Fortune 500 companies with massive advertising budgets that you'll be reading about. Rather, these are the "average joes" – just like you and me – who started from scratch, overcame obstacles, and now generate incredible seven-figure incomes!

Are you ready to embark on this exciting journey?

CHAPTER 1

MARK JOYNER:
The Godfather of Internet Marketing

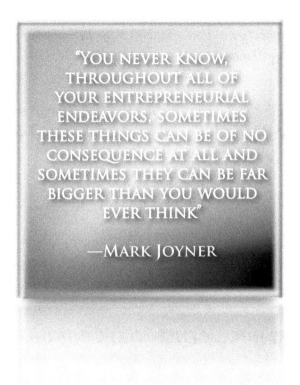

"YOU NEVER KNOW, THROUGHOUT ALL OF YOUR ENTREPRENEURIAL ENDEAVORS, SOMETIMES THESE THINGS CAN BE OF NO CONSEQUENCE AT ALL AND SOMETIMES THEY CAN BE FAR BIGGER THAN YOU WOULD EVER THINK"

—MARK JOYNER

A TRUE INTERNET SUCCESS... A TRUE MARKETING LEGEND...

They call him "The Godfather of Internet Marketing."

When he started out online, he had absolutely no idea what he was doing... what he was doing would one day revolutionize the world of Internet marketing and change the way we do marketing online forever.

Now, this individual goes down in history as one of the greatest ever Internet marketers, pioneering the world of e-commerce, and responsible for introducing many of the technologies and tactics you see on the Internet today, including e-books, remotely hosted ad-tracking, integration marketing etc.

Just a quick glance at his list of achievements will daze you:

- *The driving force behind many Top 100 web properties, including one which became the 37th most visited website on the planet within six weeks of its release*

- *Wrote a pioneering e-book (regarded as the world's first ever e-book) that was downloaded over 1,000,000 times*

- *Turned his fledgling one-man operation into a multi-million dollar international corporation with customers in every Internet-connected country on the planet*

Who is he? He's of course the one and only Mark Joyner.

In the eyes of many, Mark is regarded as a huge success, living the Internet lifestyle. Yet for him, this is only the beginning.

FROM MILITARY INTELLIGENCE TO THE INTERNET
— *"I had always wanted to be an entrepreneur"*

Stanley: I understand that you were actually in military intelligence before you got started online. Tell us a little bit about that and how you eventually got introduced to the Internet.

Mark: Sure. Yes, I was in the military at the time that I started getting involved on the Internet – actually pre-Internet. I had one of the early computers and started doing marketing over a bulletin board system, which was one of the things that were popular amongst computer geeks before the Internet was popular.

It was basically where people could call into a system that people would generally run on home PCs via a single phone line to upload, share files, and communicate via bulletin boards. It was similar to the way the Internet is run now, but far less efficient because, generally, only one person could be logged in to one of the bulletin boards at a time, or even a couple of people at once in the more sophisticated operations.

When I was working in military intelligence in the army, I was doing this business on the side just for fun. As soon as the Internet started getting a little more popular, around '93 or '94, I jumped online and immediately started playing around with selling things. I didn't realize back then how big all this was going to be.

I'd always wanted to be an entrepreneur and thought, "Well, now is the time to do this. I see an opportunity." There wasn't any rule book back then for, "How to do business on the Internet." Nobody was really doing it – it was all fresh. We didn't even have secure transactions back then, so you couldn't really pass credit card information in a secure way.

We were experimenting with all sorts of stuff. And I started coming up with my own rule book in my mind, based on my experience at studying military strategy, martial arts and human psychology. There was something that a martial arts teacher told me once, which was, "You could apply everything you learn in martial arts metaphorically to any other kind of fighting, or to business, or really to anything in life."

I thought, "If this is really true, let's test this out. I don't have a rule book for doing business on this Internet thing (which nobody really understood back then), so why don't we do the same thing?"

Some of it worked really well and some of it didn't work very well at all. It wasn't until later that I started getting exposed to more of the classic direct marketing approaches and found that some of what I had come up with was similar to that.

Some of it was violating some of those laws and doing well; some of it was violating the laws and not doing very well at all. That's the essential gist of how it happened in the beginning.

THE FIRST EVER E-BOOK

— *"I didn't realize at the time how important this would become... I didn't realize that it would be an historic event"*

Stanley: What did you do in your early days as an Internet marketer?

Mark: I was selling all sorts of little things here and there – mostly a lot of early information products and little reports. Back in the bulletin board days, you'd write up a little how-to report about something that you discovered, and you could post it up on the bulletin board and tell people, "Hey, I've got a little report that will teach you how to do X, Y, Z."

For example, I wrote up a little report for people who were interested in getting involved in military intelligence and the language training program. It was a little booklet teaching them, "If you want to be in the U.S. Military Language Training Program, this is what you have to do." And I was actually able to sell that.

It ran the gamut from a number of different things, but I didn't start getting more serious about it until I started getting into a more nichified approach of teaching people about human development. I was very interested in taking a human being to the ultimate outer reaches of their limits. I started a website called Hot Rod Your Head around 1995 or 1996 and that was the first domain I had.

I had several different websites before that that weren't on dedicated domains. Everything leading up to that had all been hit or miss. One of the things I did back then in '93 or '94 was that I wrote what a lot of people consider now to be the first e-book ever. I don't know if that's true, but it's the first time anyone had used the phrase "e-book" and it was certainly the thing that popularized it.

I didn't realize at the time how important that would become. By 1998, the e-book had been downloaded over a million times and we were starting to make inroads in the popularization of the medium. At the time, I just thought, "This is a really cool idea and I think there's a lot of potential." But I didn't realize that it would be an historic event.

You never know, throughout all of your entrepreneurial endeavors, sometimes these things can be of no consequence at all and sometimes they can be far bigger than you'd ever think.

Stanley: What was the e-book and what do you think was the major success behind it? What made it so viral?

Mark: There were several components that were really important. First of all, the newness was super important – nobody was offering e-books. It just wasn't something that people thought about. There were a couple of what people were calling "e-texts" back then that were like ASCII files, the written text from a particular document.

There was a huge difference between presenting something as an e-text, which wasn't really meant to be read or used in the same way, and an e-book, which was, "This is the format it's supposed to be in. We're not asking you to print this out; we're telling you this is what it's supposed to be." It shifted people's mentality and changed the perceived value of that text.

In terms of making it viral, the newness was important, but also the topic, the newness of the topic. The book was called *Search Engine Tactics* and was on something that simply hadn't been written about, so almost certainly that was the first book about search engine marketing and how to capitalize on the search engines to get a marketing effect.

On top of that, we employed a really interesting tactic, which would still work well today but wouldn't have the same impact because the buzz worthiness just isn't as high, and it was to make the book free and we included a little blurb on the bottom that said, "You may give this book away or even sell it by itself or part of a paid package as long as you include it intact as the 'Tactics. exe' file."

What this told people back then was something really important: People were starved for content on their web pages. It's kind of silly to think of it now and seeing how far we've come, but back then, people had web pages and even putting in a link to Yahoo.com would make the site more valuable. This was the level of sophistication people had back then, which was quite low.

So when they saw that notice on the e-book, they thought, "Wow, I can upload an e-book and my customers are going love my website, because I'm offering this free content." That allowed it to spread like wildfire throughout people who were just starting to poke around and play with entrepreneurialism on the Net.

FOREVER WEB: THE FIRST BIG FAILURE

— *"We were bouncing around from concept to concept and didn't have any one, single, unifying thing that identified us"*

Stanley: After this first e-book success, what was your next project?

Mark: It's hard to say what the very next one was. I've always been so fast, moving from place to place. One of the things I experimented with – and I don't know if I've ever talked to anyone about this, but seeing as we're going so far back, you're sparking my memory – was a terrible attempt at a website we had called Forever Web.

The idea was that you would pay a one-time fee and get a web page that would stay up forever. The fact that the website doesn't exist anymore tells you how legitimate that was! The intention was to keep it up for a long time. When we closed it down, we just told people, "Look, you can ask us for your money back or here are some alternative products and services we can give you. We're sorry we're closing this down."

People responded very well to that. They appreciated the fact that we were honest and not just packing up and leaving town, which was one of the things that I must say has probably given us a huge competitive advantage in the marketplace. It was that general sense of the positive treatment of the customer throughout the whole thing.

I think what's really interesting to note is that we experimented with so many different things and we never really slowed down. We were constantly trying new things and were never daunted by the lack of belief of someone else. I remember when e-books were first coming out, there were people who I was trying to get to buy off on the whole concept of e-books, and they would tell me, "That's just ridiculous. Nobody's ever going to buy an electronic book."

My dear friend Joe Vitale, for example, who is one of the smartest guys I know and a genius marketer – it took me two to three years to get Joe to finally say "Yes" to doing it. He had an old book called *Hypnotic Writing*, which had long gone out of print, and I said, "Just find an electronic copy of this in any format and we'll do all the work."

He finally dug it up and, because it did so well, now the whole Hypnotic Marketing franchise was rekindled as a result of that. It just goes to show that sometimes even really intelligent people won't believe in your ideas. It's no offense to Joe – he was probably super smart for turning it down, because there were so many things going on in the early days of the Net, very few of them actually stuck.

It was a good marketing decision from his perspective, but it's interesting how that dynamic plays out when you're the person who has an idea. The success of the idea is sometimes determined by your determination to make it so.

Stanley: What lessons did you learn from the failure of the Forever Web site?

Mark: I think the model was flawed. I wasn't thinking in the long term and didn't realize, at as deep a level as I do now, the value of a lifetime customer. I didn't realize that the long-term money from a customer was coming from the backend sales in that relationship. I just thought people would be so turned on by the concept of, "I pay once and pay forever." But I can keep the sales coming in.

I did realize that I would be able to sell to those people after the fact as well, so it wasn't a terrible model, but it wasn't one that I had fully committed myself to. That's a theme that probably played out over and over again, even as we achieved greater and greater success, and we were selling millions and millions of dollars in products and services.

We were bouncing around from concept to concept and didn't have any one, single, unifying thing that identified us. The new company I'm working on now called Simpleology is far more unified and far better thought out as a brand concept than any of those past ones were.

THE BIRTH OF INTEGRATION MARKETING

— *"Integration marketing was the exact same thing that allowed Microsoft to amass the greatest fortune in the history of the world"*

Stanley: What was your next step?

Mark: It's hard to say, again, because we did so many things and a lot of it just runs together. Keep in mind that I'm glossing over tons of little projects that we did and tons of really significant experiments including a lot of search engines that we started. For example, we started the second pay-per-click search engine on the Internet and the first search engine to offer child-safe searching.

It was also the first search engine to actually sell a keyword database of the terms people were searching for. It's kind of side note that I don't really talk about too much, but it was really significant in terms of what we were known for in the entrepreneurial world, the further development of our e-book publishing, and then of some really interesting services.

Probably the most significant in terms of the actual growth of our company was one called ROIbot, which was the first ever ad-tracking service on the Net. We sold that initially by itself, but then we had a profound realization that people weren't utilizing all of the real estate that they had available to them on the Internet.

I was watching something from a friend of mine, Joe Sugarman, the father of the infomercial, who was talking about how someone would call in to order a pair of BluBlocker sunglasses (that's one of his companies), and that you couldn't walk away from the telephone operator without ordering several other pair for your parents, your dog, or whomever.

He greatly enhanced his profitability by doing this. This is not a new thing; it wasn't new for him. What was new for him was the whole infomercial idea. The ideas of upselling, cross-selling, downselling, and all of that weren't new, but they were new when Joe used them for infomercials because infomercials hadn't existed.

It was new for us because nobody was really incorporating this on the Internet. When somebody would sign up for a newsletter or purchase a product, basically what people would see is, "Thank you for ordering." So one of the things we started doing was incorporating additional offers on our thank-you pages.

Now you see people talking about a lot of the tactics we used as one-time-offers. That simply didn't exist on the Net until we started incorporating those systems. After the ROIbot cross-sell on the thank-you pages of our own e-books, I started developing a concept that I realized later on was far bigger than I knew then.

That was to take that same offer and put it on the thank-you pages of the websites of other companies, selling similar things. This sounds like a very plain, vanilla thing – it doesn't sound very interesting on the surface, until you realize what it's doing for a business.

It was the single most important catalyst in the growth of the business, far more powerful than any of the viral marketing stuff that we did, in terms of growing the profitability of the business, because the viral marketing wasn't always profitable.

It's when you combine that kind of thing with the viral marketing that we were getting great results. I later realized that this same concept, that I now call integration marketing, was the exact same thing that allowed Microsoft to amass the greatest fortune in the history of the world.

SIMPLEOLOGY:
THE SIMPLE SCIENCE OF GETTING WHAT YOU WANT
— *"The shortest path between where you are right now and the things you want in your life is a straight line"*

Stanley: Throughout the years, you started moving away from Internet marketing and went into something called Simpleology. What inspired you to do that?

Mark: There were several phases there. First, I closed down all of my old Internet marketing businesses and sold off a lot of the intellectual property with this thing called The Farewell Package, which was a collection of a lot of software source code and a revealing of a lot of the tactics that we had been using over the years.

It was probably the first major high-priced product launch of its type in that particular space. We sold it for $1,000, which is quite commonplace on the Internet now, but back then people were selling stuff generally for no more than about $100 to $200, so it was really interesting on many levels.

I was working behind-the-scenes with some people as a silent partner on different projects, writing a few books, and just laying low for a while. People would pay me $2,000 an hour for consulting. I don't do that anymore, by the way; I can't afford to take that kind of money because my time is worth more.

People would pay me that money for marketing advice. And what I found, for about 90 percent of the people who called me, was that they didn't really need marketing advice. They'd already had a really high number of great ideas. What they really needed to do was start being more effective as people. I started giving them information that was a little outside of what they wanted, but was actually what they needed.

The people, of course, were extremely happy because I was solving the real problem that they saw. Over time, I started slowly developing that into a set number of rules and processes that I could give to people. I said, "I've got so many people writing in every day and asking me for help on various topics and I just don't have time to help all of these people, so I want to put this into a system where anyone can learn and benefit from it for free."

If somebody wanted help from me, I would say, "Go do this process first and if you still need my help, come back and talk to me." That became what's now Simpleology 101 and Simpleology 102.

Stanley: What is Simpleology?

Mark: Simpleology is the simple science of getting what you want. The idea is really simple, which is, the shortest path between where you are right now and the things you want in your life is a straight line. And I don't just mean the things you tell everybody you want, but I mean what you really want deep in your heart, the thing you won't tell anybody that you really want.

It's easy to just walk a straight line toward it ...

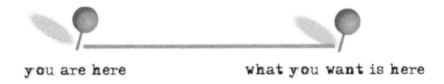

you are here   what you want is here

Source: Simpleology.com

The problem is, people simply aren't walking a straight line toward it. They're walking a wavy line or they're walking a straight line in the wrong direction. Simpleology helps you cut through all the nonsense and begin walking a straight line to those things that you want. You'll start to find that getting those things is a lot easier than you realized.

Stanley: What are the five laws of Simpleology?

Mark: The five laws are basically what we have distilled down to what we think the essence is of getting the things you want. What are the five laws you have to follow to get anything you want in your life? Just to go over very briefly what they are:

1. **The law of straight lines,** which we just talked about, and that's the shortest path between any two points, especially between what you want and where you are right now.

2. **The law of clear vision,** and that is if you don't have a clear idea in mind of what you want, you're not going to be walking a straight line toward anything. You're going to be walking a straight line in a random direction, so of course you're not going to get where you want if you can't see it clearly in your mind.

3. **The law of focused energy,** and that is if you are not feeling a real positive energy about doing something, the effectiveness of your actions toward it are going to be greatly diminished.

4. **The law of focused attention.** Obviously, if you're not paying attention to the thing you want, well, where do you tend to go in your life? You tend to move in the direction where you're paying attention and this is where all of your effort ends up. So you need to pay continuous attention to the actions required to get the thing you want.

5. **The inevitability of action and reaction,** which is probably the subtlest of the five. There is another little bit that you kind of need to know that goes along with it. Before we can understand the inevitability of action and reaction, we've got to understand that there are two questions that you're asking yourself every moment that you're alive. We call them the two most important questions of your life.

You're asking yourself this question right now, every moment that you're alive, but you're generally doing it unconsciously and giving yourself an answer too. The two questions are:

1. **"Are the actions you're taking bringing you closer to or further away from the things you want?"** It may sound like a really simple thing, and it is simple, until we realize that most of our actions are actually taking us further away from the things we want. Then we scratch our heads and wonder, "Hmm, why aren't we getting the things we want?" We're getting conscious awareness of that. It helps you short-circuit that insanity that we live through that prevents us from getting those things.

2. **"Are the actions I'm taking increasing or decreasing my power?"** In Simpleology speak, we say that the three sources of power are: Time, energy and money. Most of the actions we take are actually decreasing our power. The food we eat is often decreasing our energy. The thoughts we have often decrease our energy. The time we're spending is decreasing our time power. The money we're spending is decreasing our money power. Getting conscious awareness of that allows you to short-circuit that as well.

Once you have that and you can start to see that, now you can really understand the fifth law and that's that every moment you're awake, you are involved in some form of action, and for every action, there is going to be some kind of a reaction.

Some people might think, "What do you mean? I spend a lot of time procrastinating." Procrastination actually doesn't exist. It's a trick of the mind. It's a nonsense term and is really meaningless, because if you think about it, even if you're "doing nothing" sitting on your butt and watching TV, that is an actual activity that you're involved in.

You made a choice to be involved in that particular action and there is a huge symphony of reactions to sitting on your butt and watching television. You're being programmed by the TV to have a certain belief set which may or may not serve the things you want to attain in your life. You're sitting there, letting your muscles atrophy.

There's a whole symphony of things happening and this is true for every single thing that you do, and you're always doing something every waking moment. Once you get that realization, all you've got to do then is say, "Look, if I'm always doing something, I've just got to choose the actions that bring me closer to the things I want." And it really is that simple.

Stanley: You're a big believer in setting targets. Can you walk us through the power and process of setting targets?

Mark: Sure. If you don't have a clear target in mind, again, this speaks to the second law of Simpleology, you're moving off in sort of a haphazard, random direction. I know that there are a lot of people who now talk about just having a thought in your mind and allowing the universe to bring this to you.

I don't really know if that works. I don't know if anybody knows if that works because it's not something you can observe. But if you've got a clear target in mind and you take specific actions toward attaining that target, that is something you can know for a fact is working or not working. It's observable and I think it's very important to operate in this world on what you can observe to be true, otherwise it's a form of insanity.

It's simply a matter of seeing in your mind what you want and then creating a clear plan. Sometimes the plan isn't clear, but if you keep in mind what is clearly what you want, sometimes the plan will reveal itself, but you've got to take the action that you know you can take first.

Stanley: Can you give the URL for your Simpleology course to our listeners?

Mark: It's TheSimpleology.com. Simpleology 101 is free for anyone to try and we've got a ton of software that folks can use as well to, not just learn these ideas, but actually implement them and integrate them into their daily life.

SUCCESS IS YOUR GREATEST ENEMY

— *"I've got a strong ego and a good, strong self image, but, at the same time, I don't believe that I have accomplished even a tenth of what I want to set out to do"*

Stanley: Everybody says that Mark Joyner is a huge success. What do you define as success? Do you think you have achieved that kind of success?

Mark: I think that my own opinion of myself is far lower than what my public thinks of me. You've got to be careful about how you say that. I don't have a low opinion of myself and I don't think negatively about myself. I've got a really strong ego and a good, strong self image, but, at the same time, I don't believe that I have accomplished even a tenth of what I want to set out to do.

There are things that I have in mind to do right now that are far beyond the scope of anything I've done up to this point, and I think that's very important. Success is a very dangerous thing because sometimes when people are successful, it lulls them into a sense of complacency and they stop growing at that point. They stop improving.

They think, "Well, I've become this great success. I can now stop because everyone's got this wonderful, glowing opinion of me." And that's great. It's wonderful sometimes to hear people write in and tell you that something you did has touched their lives or that they think highly of you, but you've got to be so careful.

I'll tell you a story about two teenage girls – and you'll be surprised when you hear who these two girls were. Their level of thinking was so profound. Someone was interviewing one of these girls and asked, "You've been getting a lot of negative press in the tabloids lately. How does that make you feel?"

And the girl said one of the most profound business lessons I have ever heard in my life, "I don't pay attention to our press, be it the negative press or the positive press; we're too busy doing things."

I thought, "Wow. That's so amazing." Anyone who gets any kind of public recognition or is spoken about in public at all, getting caught up in all of that pulls them out of the loop of taking action.

Sitting there and reading your own press, be it positive or negative, does absolutely nothing at all in terms of your accomplishment – there is absolutely no impact. Do you know who these two girls were? They're teenage billionaires – Mary Kate and Ashley Olsen. Would you ever expect that kind of business wisdom to come from two kids?

Stanley: No. That's truly amazing. So you actually think that success is dangerous in a way?

Mark: It can be, depending on how you allow it to affect you. Success can lull you into complacency and get you to be inactive, but it can also make you inhuman. There are a lot of people who get some kind of public recognition and all of a sudden now they think they're above the average person.

This is a really terrible thing because it will basically destroy any relationship they have with someone else. This all comes down to basic human relationships, and it doesn't matter who you are or who you're known to be, at the end of the day, the people you have interactions with are people, and people don't like to be around someone who thinks that he or she is better than them or superior.

It's disgusting and you can't tolerate it, right? I'm sure you can probably remember some people you think are really smug and above everyone else, and you can think about what it felt like when you were around those people. It's terrible – you don't ever want to be around them anymore. Why? It's because if they see themselves as being above you, where does that put you?

It puts you below them and makes you feel like less of a person. Nobody wants to feel like less of a person. This is a way that success has really destroyed a lot of people. Not only that, but people begin to think that they're bulletproof. This is why you see so many successful people getting involved in drugs.

They go out and think the normal rules don't apply to them, so they can start shooting heroin and drinking huge amounts of alcohol or snorting cocaine, and it's going to be fine. But guess what? Their humanity starts to show itself very quickly and they become a mess.

We've seen this very recently in the very sad story of Britney Spears. She was such an amazing success, but something in her head led her to believe that she could get away with living that way and it's negatively affected her. Now, I tend to think that she's going to bounce back. People can go through down-swings and can have huge rebounds.

There are a great many stories of that happening and it's a wonderful thing, but it's better to prevent the downswing to begin with if you can, so I would just have anyone heed that. There are some people who are going to have great success, and I would just warn them that there is a huge set of pitfalls that you can fall into if you're not very careful.

SIMPLEOLOGY 102: THE SIMPLE SCIENCE OF MONEY
— *"When you're selling something to someone online, it's important to remember that you're still communicating to another human being on the other end of that"*

Stanley: What do you think are the main ingredients to success as an Internet marketer?

Mark: I'm glad you said as an Internet marketer, because if you had just said success in life, I wouldn't know how to answer that. I don't know if anybody could. Who knows what success in this life is? I suppose feeling good about yourself, having good relationships, and having love in your life are some of the most important things.

In terms of being successful as an Internet marketer, I can talk about that. If your objective as an Internet marketer is to generate money through the sale of products and services over the Internet, then we have a clearly definable thing to talk about. First of all, a lot of this is codified very clearly in Simpleology 101 and 102.

We talk about attaining any goal in 101, and then in 102 about attaining money, the raw fundamentals of that are all there. In addition to that, there are a couple of things I would want to point out from a very strict perspective of talking about Internet marketing. I would say to remember that the Internet is really nothing more than a medium of communication. Right?

People think that the Internet is this big, magical thing. Yes, there are some wonderful things going on in the Internet. Technically, it's one of the most significant advancements in the history of the planet, there is no question about that. In my personal opinion, it is the most significant advancement since the printing press. I say that without any hesitation or batting an eye. If you look at the way it's impacted the world in the last 15 to 20 years, it's not hard to understand how important it is. But it's still nothing more than a medium of communication.

When you're selling something to someone online or influencing them, it's important to remember that you're still communicating to another human being on the other end. That may sound like a really trite thing until you realize the number of ways that that idea permeates your success as an Internet marketer. Two immediate ways come to mind:

The first is the way you communicate to your prospect. The more human you can be – the more you can speak to basic human psychology, which, by the way, does not change on the Internet – the better you'll do.

The other is this: When you realize that when you're selling something to someone, that's a human being whose very course of their life can in fact be changed by the product that you're selling to them. There are products we bought in our lives –whether they are the personal development or any kind of product of that matter – which have had huge impacts on our lives.

For example, the laptop you buy, the decision for the type of software you use to facilitate the things you want to accomplish, if it impedes someone or facilitates something they want to do, it can have a huge ripple effect on their lives and the things that happen throughout their lives. The impact of that is massive.

Here's what this means to you as a marketer: The impact of word-of-mouth marketing now has accelerated to such a great degree that the past methods of making money – which I have to say in many cases were very Machiavellian, there were a lot of people who amassed great fortunes in the past by ripping a lot of people off – these methods are no longer going to work and I'll tell you why.

The backlash from that impact is going to be a lot faster and a lot surer, as the world gets more and more connected. This may sound like moral posturing, but it's really not. This is actually a very pragmatic and cold way of looking at it. You simply must take great care of your customers and respect them as human beings if you expect to stay in business long.

Here's the alternative to this. I'm going to tell you a story about something that happened in the wild, wild west back in the 1800s. There were what they called "snake oil salesmen," who would actually sell snake oil as well as a bunch of other alleged miracle cures. They would have what was called a "medicine show."

They'd roll in on a covered wagon and would have a little sales shtick, where this magic potion would cure an illness that didn't exist of a shill who was planted in the audience. Everyone would say, "My goodness, this is wonderful. I've got to buy 10 bottles." And then the medicine man would sell this bogus medicine to everyone in the small town.

Then he would pack up, leave and go to the next town. Why would he do this? He couldn't keep selling the product in that town because it was garbage. It was a total scam. If you looked at a graph of his sales where you could imagine time on the x-axis and sales on the y-axis, you would see a big, sharp spike in sales and then it would drop down to nothing.

That covered-wagon salesman would do the same thing in another town and so on, but he had to keep running away to make sales. It's really interesting because a lot of people doing business on the Internet are doing this exact same thing. Here's what it looks like on the Internet. They have a massive product launch for a product that's over-hyped, and they have a sharp spike in sales.

You can observe this by looking at the graphs at Alexa.com of most of these websites. It's especially interesting when you go to a site telling you, "We're going to teach you a viral marketing mechanism that's going to allow your message to spread exponentially, and by the end of three days, half of the Internet is going to know about it."

Funnily, you can plug that URL into Alexa.com and see either no traffic to speak of, or a big spike and then it drops down to nothing. And you think, "That's funny. If what they're doing is going to teach me to get a massive wave of traffic that never ever ends, how come I don't see that on their Alexa graph? It doesn't make any sense." I would challenge everyone to check out the Alexa graph of these sites and see what happens.

These guys will do a big launch like that. The sales will drop down to nothing, they'll take the list of people who were buyers or potential buyers and roll them into another list, and then do the same thing over and over again.

That's not a business model, that's being a covered-wagon medicine show-man. That's being a snake oil salesman. If you've got to keep running away from anything or hide your identity, that should send a big red flag in your mind that you're doing something that doesn't jive with the way the world works now.

You've got to take that customer experience, you've got to take the fact that the other person on the end of that big, long string of electrons that's looking at your message from another monitor – in the same way that you're looking at yours – is a human being. When you can really get that and feel that in your bones, the effectiveness of your business will multiply a thousand fold.

INTERNAL LOCUS OF CONTROL

– *"You need to operate under the belief that you as an individual are largely responsible for those events"*

Stanley: We are approaching the end of our time together, and I want to end this call by asking you, during those tough times throughout your career, what motivated you to carry on?

Mark: Wow, that's a great question. Like anyone, I've had many periods of tough times in my life. Everybody has a long string of great triumphs and great failures. I suppose the one thing that will really get you to pull through those moments of failure is that your willingness to pull yourself through is going to determine whether or not you stick down there or you pull yourself out. That's something that over time, I get better and better at.

When I see that I'm in a slump, I pull myself out of what is called in psychology an "external locus of control." If you have that, it means that you believe that your life is determined by things outside of you. If you have an internal locus of control, you operate under the belief that you as an individual are largely responsible for those events.

The more and more you can grasp that and start to take responsibility for that, the shorter those moments of failure will live because you'll stop seeing them as failures. You'll stop seeing them as this big, traumatic sad event and just as something for you to react to in one way or another.

GREAT SUCCESS

– *"By great success, I mean getting into the $100 million or $1 billion level"*

Stanley: Mark, I want to thank you for your time. You've provided us with some excellent advice. Do you have any final comments you want to add? Also, let us know where we can find more information about you.

Mark: The main thing we're focusing on right now is Simpleology, at TheSimpleology.com. There's free software there and a free training system and that's something we're going to be improving on again and again. I would say to just go check it out.

From a marketing perspective – I know I'm speaking to marketers here – watch what we do there and see how we take the concept of improvement and change very seriously, and think about taking that same level of dedication to your own business.

If there's something you can believe in that strongly and that you can focus all of your energy into it and continually improve, there's better chance of you having great success. By great success, I mean getting into the $100 million dollar or billion dollar level.

The million-dollar level is not so difficult to achieve these days. If you want to get to that level of great success, I think that's something that's absolutely necessary and that is something I would implore everyone to consider.

CHAPTER 2

JERMAINE GRIGGS:
Founder of HearandPlay.com

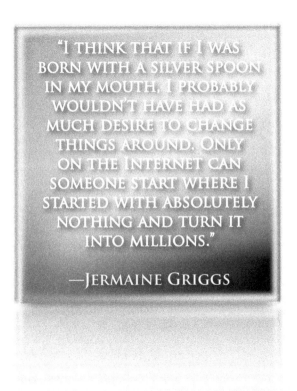

"I THINK THAT IF I WAS BORN WITH A SILVER SPOON IN MY MOUTH, I PROBABLY WOULDN'T HAVE HAD AS MUCH DESIRE TO CHANGE THINGS AROUND. ONLY ON THE INTERNET CAN SOMEONE START WHERE I STARTED WITH ABSOLUTELY NOTHING AND TURN IT INTO MILLIONS."

—JERMAINE GRIGGS

WHILE MOST KIDS AND TEENAGERS WERE ASKING FOR PLAYSTA-
tions and Nintendos, Jermaine Griggs was hooked on becoming a successful businessman and being able to afford the classic office setup one day – he was definitely not your ordinary teenager.

Growing up in the inner city of Long Beach with little money, he always had a burning desire to change things around for his family. Jermaine was always your teenage entrepreneur who envisioned life on the other side of the tracks.

At just the tender age of 10 years old, he was already knocking on doors selling products for kids through Olympia.

By 12 years old, he was selling Avon – cosmetics and perfumes – he signed his mom and grandma up in his downline.

From selling prepaid legal services to running his own stationery company... Jermaine went out and did whatever he could to change his reality. Heck, he even joined SMC products, became president for his school by 16, and launched his own website Shop2X.com.

But none of these projects produced the results he had hoped for to rescue his family from the hood. But his determination kept him going – if he just kept trying... something would pull through.

And, at 17, something life-changing happened.

On August 6, 2000, he borrowed $70 from his mom and registered the domain name HearandPlay.com and launched the company that would not only change his life, but also the lives of hundreds of thousands of musicians around the world through his books, DVDs and training courses.

Fast forward seven years to find that over two million aspiring musicians download his online lessons every year and over 245,000 loyal students receive his regular newsletters. Having seen his company grow from a few hundred dollars a month into a million-dollar business is nothing short of amazing and Jermaine is constantly reminded of his humble beginnings.

As we grill Jermaine for the next 70 minutes – his ups, his downs – we see in sharp focus what it was like to be a teenage entrepreneur. And yet this story is not just a one man's tale. It is the story of a time and place – the Internet - seen from the unique point of view of a man who knows what it feels like to be on both sides of the tracks.

A BURNING DESIRE

— *"I actually knew I was going to be a businessman at the tender age of eight years old"*

Stanley: Jermaine, can you start off with your childhood?

Jermaine: Sure. I grew up in the inner city of Long Beach, California. Some would call it the hood. It wasn't the greatest area, but it wasn't a war-zone either. It was right there in the middle.

I grew up with a single mother and my sister, and my grandma was around for most of the time during my childhood. We had a lot of care, a lot of love, we went to church, and things were great in that regard. But we didn't have a lot of money. I didn't have the name brand shoes and the Nikes. We had cable on sometimes, but then it would be cut off, things like that.

At an early age, I really got a desire. Most of you have read the book Think and Grow Rich by Napoleon Hill. I hadn't read it at eight; I hadn't read it at 10 years old. But I had this burning desire to be very successful so young because of what I saw around me. I knew that I could be the one to change the things around me.

By 10 years old, I was selling for Olympia. There was this little sales club called Olympia and I signed up for that club, which was especially for kids. You basically sell stuff out of a catalog and you get $2 or $3 per sale. I was knocking on doors and every summer I'd make $50 here, $100 if I could sell 50 items to my family or neighbors. That was a glimpse of the little bit of businessman inside of me at that age.

A year later, I remember selling Avon, which are things like cosmetics and perfumes. It's a pretty big network marketing company. I'm 12 years old and this representative is sitting in my living room. And I'm like, "Mom, can you sign me up?" So she signs me up for Avon, and because it's network marketing, she signs up in my downline, and we signed grandma up in her downline. It was so funny.

That didn't last too long, because it was hard for me to sell Avon in high school, since my guy friends would tease me, "Man, you sell perfume and stuff." And I replied, "Well I just want to sell to your parents. I don't care. Your mom could be my customer."

But at the end of the day, I went on to selling prepaid legal services – that was another network marketing company. I sold Quickstar. I bought wholesale products from this company called SMC Products. By the time I was 16, I had been through so many things I had tried in my life: From a stationery company, to connecting our bikes together and giving kids rides around the neighborhood for 25 cents in the wagon, just little things like that. I guess I was what you'd call a "hustler."

I often tell people, "I'm just like many other entrepreneurs, who skip around from thing to thing, opportunity to opportunity. The only difference in me is that I started at 10." Most people start in their 20's and 30's, thinking about life; I just started thinking a little earlier.

Fast-forward a few years later, and after trying everything I could, I considered my passion. Now, the thing about my passion is I played piano since eight years old. I've always been a piano player for the majority of my life. I wasn't just a piano player who read sheet music. In fact, even to this day, I can't read sheet music that great.

I picked up the piano on my own by just listening to songs on the radio and playing them right when I heard them. It might take me a minute or two and I'd play these songs. Naturally, I got asked to play at church and to play for the choir. After church, parents would come up to me and asked me how I learned. I told them I taught myself. Then they'd say, "Well, can you teach my kids?"

So I managed to have a good amount of students. They were my age. Some of them were older, some of them were younger. This is how I thought maybe I could make money teaching people how to play piano. It seemed too good to be true until people started paying me $10 per lesson. I wasn't making enough to treat it as a real business – $10 here, $10 there, $15 here.

But one thing that did happen, that was particularly important, was that it caused me to create this book. I said, "Well, if I'm going teach these kids, I'm not just going to talk about the same stuff over and over because that's pretty boring.

I don't want to teach Rebecca major scales, then teach John the same thing, and then if I get a new student, Chris, I've got to teach him the same thing."

I didn't know what leverage meant back then at 15 years old – that's a big word to me today – but I knew if I could make a book one time and copy it over and over at a photocopy machine, it would make it a lot easier to teach these kids. So that's what I did.

I went on Microsoft Word and created a 30-page book that covered stuff I already knew from my own mind. I had specialized knowledge; I had knowledge in a particular area. And I think everyone does. Everybody who is reading this has knowledge and specialized skill. I did and I managed to get it on paper. I got it in Microsoft Word and printed it out.

Who would have thought that, a couple years later, at the age of 17, I would have launched HearandPlay.com with this same workbook that, just a year or two back, I was teaching kids in my own neighborhood with? So, that was kind of where I've been, from young childhood to just at the break of something that was about to change my life. And that was HearandPlay.com. I registered the domain name on August 6, 2000.

THE BIRTH OF HEARANDPLAY.COM
— *"The Internet just came as the next natural progression in my life"*

Stanley: Why did you decide to sell this product through the Internet?

Jermaine: I guess you could say trial and error. While I was teaching offline, I tried a few Penny Saver ads, which is like a little magazine that comes every week, with advertisements and classified ads – kind of like your "nickel magazine" or "nickel newspaper."

I tried advertising, just spending money here and there – money I didn't have, by the way. I tried printing out flyers and putting them on people's cars. I tried going to the local Laundromat, where people wash their clothes, and putting them up at the grocery stores. I just tried all these free ways to do it that I thought naturally. I didn't have any business experience.

I thought, "Well, this is how people get the word out, right? They pass out a bunch of flyers to people who don't want them, who throw them on the ground and throw them off of their cars when they see them." And it never worked. I didn't get one sale – zilch.

Being the entrepreneur that I was, everybody now understands I was the type who, if anybody could change his circumstances and his life, it was going to be me, because I tried everything. Just look at all the things I was in. So the Internet just came as the next natural progression in my life. I saw people putting up ads on the Internet, and, for me, I said, "Well, it's worth a try."

Even prior to HearandPlay, I had delved into the Internet a little bit. I started Shop2X.com. Remember that I told you that I sold wholesale products? I found this company called SMC Products. They would sell you these products very cheap and you could go resell them. eBay was just getting started and a lot of people were doing this on eBay. So I put up a site, but it didn't do too well, it didn't make any sales.

So I knew a little bit about the Internet before I considered HearandPlay. I did some affiliate marketing at the early stages of LinkShare.com. You can go to and join to be a salesperson for some of the bigger companies out there. For example, you could go sell chocolates or Date.com and get a referral fee.

I never did too well other than one company that was willing to pay me $0.50 per click per visitor – not even for sales, just if you sent visitors. So I was like, "Well, I'm going to throw all my attention to this." So I started sending visitors to this site by posting on message boards, forums and bulletin boards. We're talking 1999 here, so we're not talking about the sites that are out today. These are like bulletin boards, groups and things like that.

I managed to get 1600 visitors to click on this link. Keep in mind, this particular program was paying me $0.50 per click, and in my account it said they owed me $800. But I thought, "This is too easy. This is per click, not per sale, not per lead. They're not going to pay me. They're going to find out that all I'm doing is posting my ad on different sites, and people are clicking, and I'm telling my parents to click."

So I just sort of gave up, because they pay every three months anyways, so I didn't expect a check. Then three months later, I got a check for $800. This was before HearandPlay.

I say all that to say that I did know the power of the Internet. I had tried affiliate marketing; I had tried different programs; I tried Shop2X.com; I had my own AOL hub. So I saw the Internet as a vehicle.

It was just a matter of finding my right place to be. But my place to be didn't come for me until I launched HearandPlay.com, and that's what I've been doing ever since. So I bounced around until 2000 and I'm happy to report that I haven't done anymore bouncing since.

Stanley: What was your first sale and how did you get it?

Jermaine: I managed to make my first sale in the first month. All I did was I put up a simple page, I put up a picture of my book using a little disposable camera, and I got it developed at the local drug store, and then I scanned it at Kinkos, which is like a copy shop. I got it uploaded on their scanner and I put up this site.

Now, I did all the wrong things. I didn't know about long sales pages; I didn't know about direct-response marketing; I didn't know about headline. I just put a picture of my site up with a few sentences, which said, "Buy my course. This course will teach you how to play piano, scales, chords, chord progressions, and you'll be playing by ear. Click here to buy." And I had a PayPal button, which was X.com back then. It wasn't even PayPal, which came a few years later.

I just started going to all those message boards and forums that were dedicated to piano. I found over 300 forums by searching Google. I put them all in my favorite places. I made accounts for all of them.

Now keep in mind, I didn't have any money, and that was my biggest challenges. So I couldn't just go out and put ads on all the popular sites. Google wasn't even all that popular back then either. You didn't have that many opportunities so I went grassroots style. I didn't have any money but I had time on my hands.

I would post on all of these forums and I would try to post in a way that didn't seem like an advertisement. But I can't say I did that in the beginning. In the beginning, I probably copied and pasted all my advertisements, and it probably got deleted by half of the moderators, because I didn't even know what I was doing.

But as I started figuring this out, I said "Wow, if I put something that sounds like it's really coming from me, people aren't deleting it." So I would have maybe 20 different messages I would save on my computer. And it's interesting, you can still do this today.

There's a program called ShortKeys, which basically lets you type in a bunch of messages and store them into this program. If I know they're asking a question about major scales, I can have this pre-programmed message.

All I'd have to type is "##scales" and the computer would type this whole thing out for me. It was an easy way for me not to have to retype everything, so every time there was something I could repeat over and over again in new forums, I'd put it in this program. For example, any time I put "##jermaine" it would give an introduction to me, like "Hi, my name is Jermaine..." You could have as many words in it as you wanted.

So, I said, "OK, so let me have a few that I could use that sound general enough that I could answer people's questions if they ask about this, or that, but mention my website in there in a way that didn't sound like an advertisement."

So I did that in the very beginning and I did that every single Saturday – it was like a ritual. I'd get out, a few hours or two, and I'd go to all the forums and I'd post. I'd message people on these forums, because those are my clients, those are my potential customers. I didn't have any money, so this was the only way to get them to my site.

Obviously, I put my site in DMOZ and every directory I could find. I submitted to all the search engines. Even back then, FreeForAll links were the big buzz, where nowadays, they're just spammed out. But, back then, you could submit your site to these FreeForAll link directories and get some nice exposure and list serves. AOL had their own list serves, for different categories, and chat rooms.

So there were all these free ways that I was forced to go. In my first month, I generated one sale and it paid for the domain name. The domain name cost me $70 and to have $70 in the bank, that was a good thing for me back then. I never kept more than $150 in the bank probably, just a little teenager, from playing at church and stuff like that.

I managed to get my website to get about 1,000 visitors in a month from all these different efforts. But my conversion rates were not that good. Sometimes I'd get 500 people to my site, or 1,000 people to my site, and I'd get about 5-10 sales per month. That's it. Not a dozen, not two dozen, not three dozen.

This happened for my entire 12th grade year in my high school before I graduated. A sale for me was about $60, sometimes $55 when I did a special. And when I get a sale, I'd just go to the local copy shop, photocopy my book, and send it out to the post office – that's how it worked. I'd get a sale maybe every other day.

Sometimes I'd go a week without getting a sale, sometimes I'd get 2 sales in a day. So it became sporadic. It wasn't every day; it wasn't a pattern or anything. But over time, the whole of 2000, I'd make $300 per month. In 2001, I'd make $300 per month. It never grew; it just fluctuated from $200 or $300. At the most, about $500 per month.

This is how I struggled, this is how I went. In the beginning, it wasn't great money that I could retire or support myself on. I didn't think of it as a business at this point. I just thought it was a cool part-time thing. I was on my way to college at the University of California. So I just kind of did this while I went to school.

It didn't get serious until I was actually in college as a freshman in my dorm room. That's when I decided, if $200 or $300 worth of people are buying from me, there's got to be more people out there with a similar problem. More people at church come up to me than people who buy my book every month, so

I know there's more people out there who want to learn piano in the way that I'm teaching it – by ear. I know for a fact. How do I attract more people? How do I get people coming to my site to buy from me?

That's when I really started studying Internet marketing and I really got serious about it. Before, I just put up my site and did some message board advertising. But now, it was about changing my site in a way that would attract more buyers and more people to take action.

FROM $300 TO $8000 PER MONTH OVERNIGHT

–   "Your treasure is already in your backyard"

Stanley: How did you discover those Internet marketing techniques?

Jermaine: What I did was I went to Yahoo!, because I didn't even use Google back then, and just started typing in "make money", "how to grow my business" just those buzz words that we all type in when we want to see what's new, what course can help us do this, or where we can find information.

I started typing in those words and I came across this guy named Corey Rudl from MarketingTips.com. I could not help but to find him. Every page I found, anything I typed about Internet marketing, this guy came up. Even when I didn't want to click on him, I'd click on someone else and I'd end up going to his site because he'd have a banner on their sites. And just the whole front page, I couldn't help but to get to his site.

So, finally, I started reading his sales page and his sales page made me feel a certain way. It was a long sales page, but I read that entire sales page from the top to bottom – that's how powerful it was. And not only did I invested the $200 to buy the course, but I said to myself, "What if I could make my customers feel the same way I feel about his product? It was a solution to my problem and my problem happened to be 'how can I grow my business' and my customer's problem was 'how can I play piano by ear.' There's got to be some secret formula."

So, when his course arrived, not only did I devour his course, but I immediately started learning about something called copywriting, which I didn't have any exposure to before this point (this was 2002): Headlines, sub-headlines, how to open up your sales page, how to open up to your customers, how to relate to your customers, how to introduce the problem, how to agitate and poke at the problem so that your customers know that it's a real problem and that they need to make a decision now or the problem's going to exist and get worse and worse – sort of like a little pain.

People buy for two reasons: Gaining of pleasure or avoidance of pain. I learned all these things that I never knew before: Features tell but benefits sell; the longer they stay, the more they'll pay; the more they read, the more they need. And these things are sticking with me now.

So I go back to HearandPlay and I'm thinking that I have to do what Corey's done with his niche. I know he's selling "how to grow your business," but if I apply some of the things he's using, I think I can change things around here. This was an epiphany and I had this same epiphany at the age of 10 when I was selling Avon. Here it comes again, but I'm a little better off now making $300 per month.

So I turned my sales page overnight from a picture and four sentences – like I told you it was before – into about a 20-page sales letter. Now that's a big change. We're going from a little paragraph to, if you printed it out, you would have 20 pages. It wasn't that I was trying to write 20 pages. There's no rule that it has to be 20 pages for you to be successful. It's just that, as I started adding all these required elements –the headline, the bullet points, the guarantee, the P.S. (post-script) at the bottom – by the time I finished, my sales page couldn't help but to be 20 pages. It was a good 10 elements that I wasn't using before that I'm now exposed to.

I redid my site and I relaunched it on March 1, 2002, and went to bed. I woke up the next morning with this new sales page. Now keep in mind that I launched it to my group. I didn't have a mailing list, I didn't have a subscriber list, but I had a Yahoo! group. And back then it was called eGroups, but I think Yahoo! bought them out. I had an eGroup and I only had about 700 piano players on it. I was a moderator so I could send emails to them, but I didn't know their email addresses. It was weird. I sent this email out on March 1, 2002.

I woke up the next morning with $550 in sales that had come in overnight while I had slept in my college dorm room. I had never even made $300 in a month, let alone $500, which was a great month. I had made that overnight. By the end of that day, I had made $1,100 selling my piano book at $55 a pop to $69 a pop, depending on the special. I had sold upwards of 15 that day – I had never done that in a month.

The next day, after all the hype had worn down, I made $300. I said, "Wow, maybe I should pinch myself so I can wake up because this is a dream." The next day, I made $290. The next day I made, maybe, $400. The next day, maybe I made only $190. So it fluctuated from the high $100s to the low $400s every single day.

By the end of that month, I had made $8,000. This was just from my sales page. I hadn't even added more traffic yet; I hadn't started list building yet; I hadn't done pay-per-click traffic; I hadn't done any SEO. It wasn't from getting more traffic, it was just from changing one thing. So I always tell people from that experience in my life: Your treasure is already in your backyard.

Then later on, I started building my subscriber list and got an autoresponder. I did search engine optimization. Then I went on GoTo.com, which got bought by Overture, which got bought by Yahoo!. I also started focusing on backend products, and the more I added, the more I made. By the end of the year, we'd done six-figures – almost $200,000 online.

That next year, we almost doubled our revenue. I created an office. I started hiring people. It grew so fast. That next year, I was up to $45,000 per month when I launched my second product. Now, people were hungry for more and more products. I started building my name. It was that "M" word – momentum. One thing led me to another.

That first $8,000 month was great. I blew my money a lot back then. I was so excited to make all this money that I started spending it, going on trips, and buying all my dream stuff. And finally when I did get focused again, I started taking that money I was making and I started investing it back in so I could advertise.

I never touched the message boards again, not that the message boards never worked. They were great for the $300 per month life I had. But now that I was up to making about $8,000 to $10,000 per month, I didn't have that amount of time. Now I have money, I'd rather do paid advertisements over free advertisements any day, because with the paid kind, you can snap your finger and have traffic in five minutes.

THE FOUR Ps
— *"It's my passion, whether I make money at it or not"*

Fast-forward a couple years now, we're making millions of dollars online. And what are we doing? We're teaching people how to play piano by ear. And to be honest, we really focus on gospel music by ear.

So our niche is so small, so obscure, so weird, and so strange that you wouldn't think that you could make seven-figures per year teaching people how to do it. I look for the four Ps when trying to find a niche:

1. **Passion.** Is there passion in the niche? Yes, there's passion in playing piano.

2. **Patience.** They know they're not going to be a master piano player overnight, they know they have to work at it, and that your products help get them that much closer, so you can keep selling them products. It's not that after they buy this first product they're going to be a master pianist. They know they need to keep buying and investing in themselves. That's a great niche to be in where there's patience.

3. **Progression.** They know that over time, they'll get there. That's similar to patience, but there's a natural progression. So after they buy my beginner course, now they're passed it, then they buy my intermediate,

then they buy my advanced. Then they can learn gospel music, then they can learn jazz, then they can learn rock.

So there needs to be progression, a sense of one step after another that they can take. I've learned that 33 percent of customers will buy from you again. That's why backend products are so important. I didn't know this stuff when I was just getting started, but now I do. So these are some of the things that I'm applying to my business over time.

4. **Positivity.** Yes, you can make money with pain. Yes, there are ways for people to make money healing and helping people get rid of their diseases, things where people are in a really bad situation and you help them out of it, or situations where people have lost money, or want to save on their taxes, or things where they're going through negative things.

That's great, but I try to be in positive niches, where I know my products are helping them to be something positive and I don't really have to worry about the pain element, even though you can earn more money getting people to avoid pain than helping them gain pleasure.

But I like the pleasure thing. I like to be happy. I like to work with people who are happy. I like to know that if we all got together in the conference room, we'd all be happy. Not a bunch of people ranting about how their spouses left them or how to get back at your spouse. That is a niche, but it's just not a niche I would enjoy being in.

So I looked for the four Ps and luckily I found that. When I found the four Ps, obviously it's been something I've stuck with over time. For the rest of my life, hopefully I'm teaching piano. Yeah, I do other things, I teach Internet marketing, I do real estate, but at the end of the day, my passion is always going to be there. It's my passion, whether I make money at it or not.

What do you do that you'd love to do regardless of whether you'd make money? Your skills, your passions, things you love to do, things you know exceptionally well, things that people call you about. They ask you for advice on this topic. These are good candidates for niches you should try to explore and do them online.

THE LAUNCH OF NITTYGRITTYMARKETING.COM

– *"Nine out of 10 businesses fail within the first five years. We're going on eights years. That's because we provide value and people keep coming back time and time again"*

Stanley: You recently entered the Internet marketing niche, teaching others how to imitate your online success, by launching a membership site called NittyGrittyMarketing.com. Can you tell us a bit about that? What inspired you to create that membership site?

Jermaine: I've always I considered myself an Internet marketer since 2002 when I started learning about it. I just applied Internet marketing strategies to the piano niche. So I'd get asked to consult with people and I'd go speak. People would invite me to speak at their workshops, but I didn't have anything to sell or offer people. I would just speak to tell my story.

Then, finally, it occurred to me that, "Jermaine, you have so much knowledge and wisdom to share with people out there that you've learned, not by teaching people how to make money, but you've learned in your piano niche. And if anybody is qualified to teach people how to make money online, it's you, because you started in such an obscure niche where, if you take one of these experts and so-called gurus, they wouldn't be able to make one dime in my niche."

I built a list of 245,000 musicians, who want to play by ear. Now that's a pretty big list for such a niche as this. There are a lot of strategies, concepts and techniques that people can learn from hearing it from someone who has done it with no money to start, no background and no experience.

So that's what NittyGrittyMarketing does. It takes you step-by-step, behind-the-scenes with my businesses, and shows you exactly how to get started, even if you're a newbie. And if you're not a newbie, we have expert sections if you're already making money. We cover a plethora of topics from traffic, to conversion of visitors, to building a list, to following up with your people, to community building, to web 2.0 traffic strategies. We've broken the membership site into four main areas:

1. **Videos,** where you actually get to see my screen step-by-step
2. **Audios,** where you can listen to interviews, like this one
3. **Live trainings,** where I'll do question and answer calls and live webinars
4. **Documents,** like PDFs, presentations and powerpoint slides

It's a very active community and we've got tons of people who are just very excited about what we're doing. We've got thousands of members on there and we let people get started for $2.97. It's a no-brainer – you can't afford not to try it out for that amount. That's less that a hamburger meal for something that can potentially change your life.

Remember what happened for me. It was one change back in 2002 that did it for me. I'm so crazy to believe that one change is all it takes to get you building that momentum that you need. If you do not remember anything else from this interview, just remember that if I can do it, I think anybody can get online and start making money online whether it's a couple hundred dollars per month or a full six-figure business.

I think the Internet has something for everybody. If you can get in where you fit in, find a passionate niche and be able to give great solutions with value – not just some content you've gotten from other people but really try to provide value to your niche – you'll succeed.

Nine out of 10 businesses fail within the first five years. We're going on eight years. That's because we provide value and people keep coming back time and time again. That's what I'm going to teach you how to do with NittyGritty-

Marketing.com. You get right down to the details, step-by-step, from me, inside of my HearandPlay business. So that's what NittyGrittyMarketing does.

HOW TO STAY FOCUSED...
EVEN IF YOUR MODUS OPERANDI SAYS YOU CAN'T!

— *"It's almost like your goals become your passion, and when your goals become part of your passion, you can't help but to reach them"*

Stanley: How do you stay focused and not get distracted?

Jermaine: I took a test called Kolbe.com. I recommend that everybody go take that test. It's not a personality test; it's not an intellectual test; it's an instinctual test. It tells you what you do by instinct. What is your modus operandi? What it told me is that I'm not one of those kinds of guys who can just have a structured day, otherwise I'd go crazy. I believe it.

It told me that I thrive off interruptions, and that sure is right, because sometimes I open my email and I know I have three things to do, but I'll go and check other things. So I understand that weakness about myself. I understand that I can be all over the place at times.

So the one thing that has kept me focused with HearandPlay is that it is my passion. I can never leave my passion or I'm forsaking a very big part of my life. Music is very important to me so that keeps me focused as well.

But really, it's all about written goals, and I know not everybody writes goals and focuses on them. I carry this black book and I list everything I have to do, even the new ideas I need to implement.

That really helps me. I write down where I want to be one year from now, where I want to be five years from now, where I want to be 10 years from now, 15 years, 20 years, and I even have 30 years in there. Most people can't even think past five years and here I am thinking about where I want to be when I'm 50 years old.

Some things that are in there include Senator of my State in government. That's one of my 20 to 30 year goals. It's in my black book. And because I put my mind on it, I attract that kind of energy into my life. I put it out there and that's how the universe works. I'm a Christian and I believe in the law of attraction. But even before all this talk about *The Secret* and the law of attraction, that kind of stuff was already in the Bible, "As a man thinketh in his heart, so is he."

So I have always been the type to think about where I want to see myself in the future, and if you keep your mind on it every day, you can't help but do things that align with it. You're not going to do counterproductive things that take you away from your goals if you keep your goals fresh in your mind.

Another thing my family and I did was called a visualization board. What we did was take a big old white board and took a bunch pictures from magazines that we wanted our future to look like: From health, to beautiful family, to a car, a house, anything about our lives, any word that describes what we wanted in the future. And we made this big old collage on a white board with all these images from magazines, and we laminate it. It's up on my wall in my office, so I can look at this imagery and I can keep my mind focused. You can see it on my MySpace Page at MySpace.com/IslandBrown.

On my screen saver are items I want to attract into my life in my future. I know whenever I'm lagging and that screen saver goes on, if I'm looking at a screen saver it means I'm sitting in front of a computer either not doing something or I've come back to my computer and it reminds me right when I sit down to the computer.

If your screen saver is your favorite song or some kind of photo slide of yourself, that's great, but I choose to make my screen saver certain things. It can be a new house, it could be a neighborhood, it could be anything I want to attract into my life in the future, I make it as my screen saver and my desktop. If you look on my desktop right now, it's a beautiful mansion on there and these are just ways subconsciously to keep you focused on your goals.

But it really goes back to writing things down and rehearsing your goals. Now, I can't say that I say my goals out loud verbally every single day in front of the mirror like I've seen in some courses, but I can say that there's not a day that goes by that I don't sit and daydream, whether it's on my way to bed or naturally sitting in the car. I'm always thinking of the future.

If you put your mind on something or you put your energy on something so much like this – and I'm not talking temporarily when you get pumped up. I'm talking about daily, it's a part of you – you can't help but to attract this stuff into your life.

I know people don't want to hear anything so spiritual like this, but it's is a big part of my life and I have to talk about the fact that when you put your mind on something, the focus comes, the help comes. It's such a part of me. It's almost like your goals become your passion, and when your goals become part of your passion, you can't help but to reach them.

MAKE IT HAPPEN!

– *"There's nothing stopping you from success or getting to that next level even if you're already successful... but you"*

Stanley: Jermaine, I want to thank you for your time. Are there any final comments you want to add, or let people know about your main websites where they could get more information about you?

Jermaine: Well, head over to NittyGrittyMarketing.com. You can always email me at Jermaine@NittyGrittyMarketing.com, that's my private email. And head over there and give it a try. I'm not here to sell you a membership. I'm here to encourage and inspire you first and foremost. I will end by saying that there are three types of people:

1. Those who make things happen
2. Those who watch things happen
3. Those who are wondering what the heck just happened

You don't always want to be wondering what happened. These are people who say, "I wish I invested in Microsoft in the 80s." I wish, I hope, I should've, I could've, I would've. Excuses, excuses, excuses.

Don't wonder what just happened. Don't watch things happen. Yes, it's easy to watch people like me, and people on TV, and celebrities. We live in such a celebrity world where you can go pick up a magazine and wish you were them, and watch them make things happen and live out their dreams.

But you know what? Make things happen. Vow to yourself that you can be the one to make things happen. You're not an exception; you're not an exemption. You can make things happen. There's nothing stopping you from success or getting to that next level even if you're already successful, but you. There's nobody in your way but you. That's what I realized.

There's nobody in my way but me. There are people who look like me, talk like me, regardless of age, background, religion, social, economical status. There are people who look like me that have succeeded, so why not me?

And when you can answer that question honestly, you'll get yourself up, you'll get pumped, you'll get driven, you won't have any excuses, and you won't blame it on other people or circumstances. These are their excuses and things that stop us from getting to the next level.

So, remember these three kinds of people and vow to be no one less than somebody who's going to make things happen.

CHAPTER 3

TOM BEALS:
VP of Operations for MikeFilsaime.com

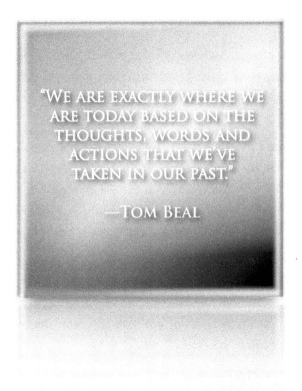

"WE ARE EXACTLY WHERE WE ARE TODAY BASED ON THE THOUGHTS, WORDS AND ACTIONS THAT WE'VE TAKEN IN OUR PAST."

—TOM BEAL

BORN TO A 17 YEAR-OLD MOTHER AND A 19 YEAR-OLD FATHER… *suffered through four divorces and six marriages of his parents as a young child…went to nine different schools by the time he was in the eight grade…*

This was the childhood life of Tom Beal – he pretty much grew up in a welfare environment. Just imagine, how could anyone, whose life was bombarded with insurmountable obstacles, negativity, tragedy, emotional pain, incredible loss... be successful?

But failure was not the case for Tom. Through his success magnet principles, he was able to become a National Bicycle Champion (now known as the X-Games), an honors graduate from the U.S. Marine Corps Boot Camp and the number-one salesperson in five separate sales organizations.

Just as he reached the top, disaster struck, however.

On a normal day in 1998, Tom was in a car crash... the car tumbled four times and he was ejected from the sunroof. He ended up in the hospital completely paralyzed, with severe head injuries. And the doctors said:

"You will never walk or talk again..."

Wrong on all accounts, Tom not only recovered from this seemingly impossible accident and learned to walk and talk again, but also became an inspiration - helping others turn their dreams into reality – the very reason why he was put on this earth.

Today, Tom is the VP of operations for MikeFilsaime.com and also a master of assisting people in reaching the top. He has worked with some of the leading people in his field, including NFL Hall of Fame Quarterback Jim Kelly, best-selling author Jeffrey Gitomer, Dr. Joe Vitale, and numerous millionaire marketers. Tom is a successful personal and business development consultant and conducts powerful live presentations.

As the familiar voice of Tom Beal chimed over the phone, I finally understood just what an incredible human being he is – his story is so mind-blowing and inspiring, you are happy to keep your own problems that you are currently dealing with in your life.

Tom is simply one in a million – just like a chapter out of the X-Files.

A TOUGH CHILDHOOD

— *"It doesn't matter where you came from or where you are now, there are steps which you can take to get to where you want to be"*

Stanley: Tell us a bit about your life and background and how you were able to overcome the difficulties.

Tom: Sure. For those who have heard or those who haven't heard, I'm just going to briefly recap the first 35 years of my life. I turned 35 a couple months ago, so if you rewind 35 years ago to 1972, I was born to teenagers. My mother was 17; my father was 19. Obviously having a kid so young was a little obstacle right from the get-go, but they tried to make things work.

They actually married and divorced twice. They got married, they divorced; they got married again, they got divorced again, and were trying to make it work, but it didn't. To make a long story short, while I was growing up, I lived around four divorces and six marriages between my two parents, so that was an interesting experience. I got to see and understand how similar circumstances can occur and people will respond differently.

That's when I realized that you can choose how to respond to your circumstances. I've seen different interactions of the multiple families that I was a part of. If you also look at part of that divorce moving-around process, I went to nine different schools by the time I was in the eighth grade. So I was always the new kid in school, always not knowing friends or having friends for a long period of time. I'd just get to learn everybody's names and then we'd move away again.

On top of that, we were pretty much in a welfare environment. We didn't have much income, but I will say we did have the love at home and we did have support at home. One of the support figures in my life growing up was my grandfather. My grandfather owned a hardwood floor company and, later on, became a home builder.

I learned a lot of work ethic from him and a lot about taking responsibility of going above and beyond the call of duty, taking pride in what you do. He provided a lot of guidance and leadership. My mother being 17 when I was born, he wasn't that much older. He was just about 40 when I was born. So he pretty much could have had a child like me of his own but it was his grandchild.

If we move forward through all those different things, I ended up being in college for a little while. I was 17 years old when I went in college, I chose the wrong crowd and instead of going to class, I would sleep because my friends and I would be out partying a lot the night before. I ended up dropping out of college after my third semester and really not knowing what to do.

I worked in a factory for a little while and then wondering through the mall on the way to my second job, a Marine Corps recruiter came up to me and asked me a question and it must have been a bad day. He said, "Are you happy in what you're doing?" At that point in my life, I really wasn't happy with the way things were turning out. I thought I'd have accomplished much more by then. So I went and talked with him.

The next thing you know, I'm in Marine Corps boot camp in Parris Island, South Carolina for three months, from January of '93 to April of '93. I ended up becoming the platoon honor graduate and was leading that platoon of about 80 people and we won all the awards and it was a great experience but it was very difficult.

Then I spent four years in active duty in the Marine Corps as a primary marksmanship instructor and also a HAWK missile systems operator, and then, halfway through, I was also a wrestler down in Quantico, Virginia, for a short period of time.

So I was in the Marine Corps, but there were some events that happened there that made me realize it was a good four-year learning experience, but I had better things to accomplish in the world as well. So after my four years of active duty, I got out and went back to college, got my Associates Degree and began my career in sales.

In sales, I applied some principles we'll probably get into today that allowed me to become number-one in five separate sales organizations. Those same principles allowed me to become an honors graduate in boot camp. Something I forgot to mention is when I was a child, around a junior or senior in high school, I was the national bicycle champion.

So the few principles that I applied to become the national champion, the honors graduate in boot camp, the number-one in those five separate sales organizations are what we will be discussing today to allow people to understand how it doesn't matter what obstacles or adversities you have faced or are facing now, there are steps you can take today that can guide you toward accomplishing your dreams and goals.

That's a quick summary. In 2001, I was online and doing some research when I heard of this gentleman named Corey Rudl and startled, "Wow, I didn't know you could do stuff like that and get great results online." So it piqued my interest and I started studying Internet marketing intensely. I also started attending live events and that's how, through networking and meeting some friends, I became VP of Operations for Mike Filsaime.

I also have a couple websites of my own that provide value to people in a couple different markets. My goal is to help people recognize that it doesn't matter where you came from or where you are now, there are steps which you can take to get to where you want to be.

SUCCESS MAGNET SYSTEM:
THE SIMPLE FIVE-STEP STRATEGY TO ULTIMATE SUCCESS

— *"Whatever the mind can conceive and believe, it can achieve"* (Napoleon Hill)

Stanley: You mentioned the principles people should follow to become successful. What are those principles?

Tom: The way I came up with them was through intense research. I'd been studying personal development intensely since 1990 when I was in college, the first semester. I had a job interview for Vector Marketing Corporation, which sells CUTCO Cutlery. I went there and I got the job. I was 18 years old selling door-to-door CUTCO Cutlery. These cutlery sets cost $800 back in 1990, so it wasn't a small investment. It was a decent chunk and I was making good money at 18 years old.

One of the keys to success that I found was studying sales and people like Zig Ziglar, Brian Tracy in the personal development arena. That led me to start studying Tony Robbins, Wayne Dyer and people like that. From 1990 to 2001, I was studying intently all the books, going to the seminars, listening to the audios and watching the DVDs.

On September 11, 2001, the event that happened in New York City really opened my eyes. I was in Charlotte, North Carolina and I remember driving south on Route 77 and hearing the news on the radio that morning as I was going to my first sales appointment. I pulled over to the side of the road and my sister called me. She was watching on TV.

Even though I've had a couple near brushes with death, that was my opener to say, "Don't wait any longer to take action that you know needs to be taken, and follow your passions." Here I was in a sales job that was working me at least 60 to 80 hours per week.

I thought it was time to start putting in action a program that would answer a question that a lot of people were asking me, "How do you do it? It seems like everything you get into, you're able to rise to the top very quickly." So I asked myself that question, "How did I do it?" Looking back, how did I become the national bicycle champion? How did I become the number-one honors graduate in boot camp? How did I become number-one in five separate sales organizations?

My mind's first response was an answer that I didn't quite like. My mind said, "There are too many different things. I can't narrow it down." So I asked myself, "If I had to narrow it down to five things that I applied in each of those areas – a lot of them deal with knowing nothing in that arena to becoming number-one in a short time – what would those five be?"

That's when I came up with the Success Magnet System. As I mentioned, it's a result of all of my studies in personal development from 1990 to 2001 – that's 11 years worth of study of people like Tony Robbins, Brian Tracy, Jim Rohn and everybody in that arena. I came up with five steps:

1. **Vision.** I always had a vision. For instance, when the bike-riding scenario happened, I saw someone doing tricks and I said, "Wow, I want to do that." When I heard Zig Ziglar speak on stage, I said, "Wow, I want to do that." When I saw the results that were happening online, I said, "Wow, I want to do that."

So first of all, I had a vision. The vision for me was seeing someone accomplish something and thinking, "Wow, that's exactly what I've been looking to do, and that just feels right. I know I'm supposed to be doing that." That's pretty much where I started. I remember going to the Marine Corps, not knowing how to march or anything.

But there were people who were in JROTC prior to going to boot camp, which prepares people in high school and some prep schools on how to march and things like that, so when I saw them doing that, I said, "Wow, I'd like to be like that." So the first step in the Success Magnet System is having that vision.

2. **Belief.** I have belief in myself and belief that if I took the same steps those people took, I too could accomplish similar results. If I put my best foot forward, chances are I'll pick it up right away, but if I keep pursuing it, I can. So you need belief in the law of cause and effect, belief in yourself, belief in your product or service and all of that.

You also need the belief that, "If that person can do it, I can too." Sometimes physical and other limitations apply. My brother is a professional football player, and for me to believe that I could do that, I could believe all I want, but he's 330 pounds and I'm not! You have to have belief in reality in certain circumstances. So as long as the belief is in line with what your strengths and abilities are, you can take the next steps.

3. **Identify and align.** Some people call it modeling or mentoring. I think "identify and align" clearly states what you want to occur. You need to

identify who has accomplished what you'd like to accomplish and do your best to align yourself with them.

I'm actually doing some of that right now in one of my favorite places, which is a bookstore. I went to Barnes & Noble to grab some coffee and wander around and see what I can find.

It's funny because now when I go to the business section, I know and I'm good friends with all these best-selling authors, so it's pretty cool. Sometimes I'm actually mentioned in their books. That's where you can align yourself. If you can identify someone and say, "Here's my goal; I have a vision; I know I can do it. I know that if I follow the same steps and have the belief in the law of cause and effect and in myself and the skills I bring to the table, I can accomplish similar results."

Who's done it? Who has performed well and is now where I want to be? How can I align myself with them? You can find them in books, audio tapes, videos, or through Google. Type in your keywords and find out who the experts are in that area. You'll find stories, newsletters, and helpful information to guide you along in the process.

4. **Commitment to action.** You have where you are and where you want to be. Through the third step, you find people who has gone from were where you were in similar circumstances, and have gotten where they are now, which is where you want to be, and figure out that they took a series of steps. It really boils down to whether you're committed to taking the proper action steps.

It doesn't happen overnight. I didn't become a national bicycle champion overnight; I didn't become number-one in the sales organizations; I didn't become the number-one honors graduate in the Marine Corps boot camp overnight. It takes hard work, dedication, discipline, and following a commitment to taking the proper action.

I emphasize the word "proper" because everybody can be busy, but you need to make sure that you're taking the proper steps that take you from where you are to where you want to be. In many cases we already know what those steps are, but then you talk about the excuses for why you aren't taking them. It takes that commitment to taking those proper action steps. Rome wasn't built in a day, and neither were successful businesses or dreams realized in one day, but you need to take that proactive step each day.

If you're not in the best of health right now, and you commit to going to the gym three to five times a week, and doing the proper action steps while you're there, chances are in six months, you'll be in better shape than you are now. That's just common sense. Similarly, in business or in any other goal that you have, if you take committed and persistent steps, you will get to where you want to be.

Stanley, you and I are halfway across the world right now, but if I were to get on the road and start walking toward the sea, and then find a boat heading in the right direction, I would eventually get there. It would take a long time. It takes a long time to get there by flight. I've flown all over the world this past year, and even had three-day travel times because of typhoons and all sorts of crazy things.

Sometimes, it takes a while to get from where you are to where you want to be. Just like with traveling, there are certain ways of getting there that will get you there eventually, they may not be the fastest way, but when you rely on the proper people, they can educate and show you how to get from where you are to where you want to be in a much quicker way, saving you the pitfalls, saving you the detours, because they've been down that path, they've walked that road, and they know how to point you in the right direction.

That's where mentoring comes in so big; that's where "identify and align" comes in; that's where you have to find and actually talk and work with those people one-on-one to have a mentoring relationship. Nothing can beat that. They can pull you and save you decades on your travel time. From the high up level where they are, they will pull you from where you are to where they are.

5. **Having Fun.** I call it the secret step. We've all heard that it's not the destination; it's all about the journey. Don't get all caught up that, "If this happens or when I get there, then I'll have fun and be happy." Or, "There's no time to be happy now." No, it's the journey. It's such a secret step.

If I look at my brother's super success in the National Football League, he enjoyed every step of the way. He enjoyed pee-wee, he enjoyed high school football, he enjoyed college football, and took those extra steps to become drafted into the National Football League.

But it didn't end there. He took additional steps to become the leader of the team, the leader of the defense. It takes that extra initiative and having fun along the way. He's being paid millions of dollars to do something he really likes. Similarly, that's what Mike Filsaime and I are doing, and many other people are doing online. We love it so much and we have so much fun.

You're going to want to write this down on a separate sheet of paper. Write down "as is." That's where you are. Then write down "should be." If everything worked perfectly, where would I be? In between the "as is" and "should be", that's the gap. It's your job to take the commitment to action and follow the steps that you know you should take to get from where you are to where you want to be.

Whatever goal you set, if you're intent on it, you're passionate about it, you have the proper skills, and if you can find a mentor to help you to tell you where you want to be, that's a done deal. Time will catch up with you. It may take six months or three years, but time will catch up and bridge that gap.

And before you know it, you're there and you'll say, "Wow! That was a fun journey." Here's the cool part. Anytime you get to the end of that journey and you've enjoyed the whole process, then it's time to set your sights on the next mission. Ships rarely sail from one port to the next and say, "Cool. I'm done. I retire." They go from that port to the next port, but they've always got that next destination, that next course to sail.

Similarly, in our lives, we're no different. If you were to look back on your life, you will see how far you've come. You've accomplished some great things already. You don't have to be monumental, but you've done some great things.

It really, truly lives up to Napoleon Hill's quote that, "Whatever the mind can conceive and believe, it can achieve." It doesn't pay to accept limits. It truly is a good saying, and that's a good quote as well. As I think it, so shall it be.

That just opens up the doors to you being the creator of your future. If I can be, do and have everything I want, what would that be? The more precise you get in detailing exactly how you want it, the more clear your blueprint is for everything to fall into place, in reality.

It's truly amazing. As you start to grasp it, set small goals, and you accomplish it following these steps, it adds reinforcement to this. And then you start to get excited, you say, "Wow! I'm the only limiting factor in where I am right now." It gives you full responsibility and full ownership.

We're in a world right now, especially in the United States, where people like to place blame on anything and anybody, "The reason I'm not there, or the reason for this is because of that person, this circumstance or that…" We are exactly where we are today based on the thoughts, words and actions that we've taken in our past.

That's the bottom line, and we will be treated five years from now exactly where we are based upon the thoughts, words and actions that we take today. If you start taking actions, start fresh today thinking, saying and doing the right things, time will catch up to you. You'll wake up and you'll go, "Wow!" The hopes that you had will all become reality.

TRAFFIC, TRAFFIC, TRAFFIC!
— *"On the Internet, it's qualified traffic, qualified traffic, qualified traffic"*

Stanley: Absolutely. I totally agree with you. When you started out in Internet marketing, what obstacles did you initially face and what motivated you to continue?

Tom: That's a good question, Stanley. I had a really good idea back in 2001 or 2002. My first site was called SetTheExample.com. It was about how we all can set the example in our own field and in our own lives. I'm trying to give some personal development strategies and motivation for people to take responsibility, set the example in their lives, and to make a commitment to setting that example.

I paid a whole bunch of money to have someone build the site, and the site looked great. I was happy the day it launched, but I kind of had the mentality that, "If you build it, they will come," from Field of Dreams. I thought, "Great. The site is live." And then I didn't get any traffic, except the traffic from family that I had sent.

I had the site. I paid money for it, and I thought, "Now I'm online. The golden road is laid out in front of me now." But that's not how it works, because there are definitely strategies and processes that have to take place in order to be able to provide extreme value to my marketplace, to make it known to that marketplace, and then also have qualified traffic there, and also the proper conversions – what actions you want them to take.

Sometimes, the action is just an opt-in. Sometimes, the action is purchasing a product. You need to be very clear on all of those, but my eagerness, with my lack of experience or knowledge in the proper way to do it, was not up to par. The site started, and I did nothing more to draw in other people than those who stumbled across it in the desert.

You can have the best store in the world, and it can be a Wal-Mart, a bookstore, or whatever it is, but if you build it in the middle of the desert, how much value are you going to provide to that marketplace? You need to make sure your business is down the street. It's about location, location, location.

On the Internet, I would say it's qualified traffic, qualified traffic, qualified traffic. How can you get the proper qualified traffic to be aware that your site even exists, and then once they get there, they will say, "Wow! This is what I've been looking for." That's the ideal scenario.

If you are able to provide those "wow" factors, you provide a true value for that marketplace and fill a void that's there in that marketplace. You've got to take a look at each of your niches, and say, "OK. Here's where that niche is right now. Here's the value I want to provide to that particular area, but where is the gap?"

What dimension can you add from the information that's already been provided? In any industry, there's already information out there. The reason new books keep coming out is because it's being fed in a different way, or they're stretching one more point in a different manner.

So, what's your difference? What's your unique selling proposition, so that when your qualified target market gets there, they don't yawn and say, "Well, I've heard that before or I've seen that before." They should actually say, "Wow! This is what I've been looking for; this is an eye opener; this is exactly the value that I was searching for." If you can do that, it's a matter of capturing that excitement, and then there are different processes you can put them through.

THE BIRTH OF BUTTERFLY MARKETING

— *"If you go with a partner to push you, you exert yourself that extra mile. That's what happened when Mike and I were working together"*

With Mike Filsaime, we've learned that our initial goal in many of the sites we do is to get them to trade their name and email for something of value. Just to get the opt-in, we give them something extremely valuable that they would have to pay for otherwise.

Many of our competitors are selling stuff like that, so we give it to them for free. And then once they give us their name and email, then we tell them if they liked that, they're really going to like this special package we put together, this special one-time offer.

We've had a lot of success in building lists and converting people from opting-in to being congruent with their initial sale. If they are willing to trade their name and email, if they liked that information that had been provided, they'd really like this special opportunity to save a good amount of money by taking advantage of this one-time offer.

Whether they say, "Yes" or "No" to that, then we also incorporate word-of-mouth. We also incorporate tell-a-friend technology, "Who else do you know who would be happy to get that free gift you just got? By the way, they will also see the offer that you saw. When they choose to buy it, you'll earn 50 percent of that sale, so that on a $97 sale, you'll earn $48.50."

There's a vested interest in them telling their friend, other than just being good hearted. Now, birds of a feather flock together. That's just how restaurants and certain stores get business from word-of-mouth referrals; that's how things spread quickly and virally online.

You can get your site viral by getting people to sign up thinking they already got value, and then tell their friends about it. That's how Gmail and Hotmail spread, by word-of-mouth, through viral technology or the viral aspect, to help the word get spread for you based upon your current customers telling their friends, and people will buy it.

Stanley: Basically, that's Butterfly Marketing?

Tom: Yes, the Butterfly Marketing process works extremely well for Mike and myself, and many other people. We also see a lot of people doing other things that you wouldn't recognize as Butterfly Marketing. That's a simple sales process that we put people through, starting off with a free or better offer and then putting them through that funnel.

There's something right away. We launched The 7 Figure Code on July 7, 2007, and that didn't have an opt-in process. That just went direct to that page. There are a bunch of different strategies that you can implement to get the opt-in and/or to get the sale on that initial page.

Stanley: Speaking of Butterfly Marketing, can you tell us the story behind it? When and how did you meet up with Mike?

Tom: Butterfly Marketing came out on January 31, 2006. Mike and I met in January of 2005. Initially, we met in passing at Stephen Pierce's event called Unleash Your Marketing Genius in Detroit, Michigan. We didn't really connect then. We just said, "Hi" in passing, traded names, emails and business cards.

After that event, one of the few that I did, in January of 2005, I had this cool video technology for which I paid a couple thousand dollars. It had my logo on it. At the time, my site was TheSalesChampion.com. My business card was eye-catching. It looked like a super hero caricature of me. I had on a Superman cape, flying through the air. It was a drawing, a cartoon caricature, but it looked like me.

Number one, the card that I handed to people was eye-catching and memorable. Number two, everybody I met at the event went straight to video. Video in January 2005 was still fairly new, not many people were doing it at all. I put a video email together, and that caricature from my business card is in the corner. Half of the page was the caricature, and half the page was the video. It was memorable.

Mike remembered it and said, "Well, that's pretty cool." That was the same time that Alex Mandossian and Armand Morin released Instant Video Generator, so that was done. I already had the technology that had cool video email, so that was memorable.

Fast forward a couple of months. Mike and I ran into each other again at an event in San Antonio in March of 2005. It was Joel Christopher and Ted Nicholas' Double Birthday Blowout. It was kind of by coincidence. It was just put yourself in that environment and be observant for the current draw. I plugged in on the side wall.

If you bring a laptop, there are not plugs all over the place. Generally, you have to search for an outlet to plug your laptop in. I was already plugged in and saw this gentleman walking around looking for a plug. I saw him looking around and said, "Hey, if you want, we can share this plug right here."

So, he sat down and it was Mike. We started chatting. We didn't really talk much business. We were just getting to know each other and hanging out at the event. We went afterwards to the River Walk with Dan Tony, because he'd already gone to the Alamo. I said, "I missed the Alamo." So he gave me a tour of the Alamo.

We became good friends, and, afterwards, we stayed in touch. And I invited him to come meet a friend of mine who's a best-selling author, Jeffrey Gitomer. Jeffrey had some goals online, and I said to him, "I'm finding a lot of people doing some great things online. How about we set up a meeting at your office in Charlotte?" I invited Mike Filsaime, Brad Fallon, Paulie Sabol and myself. We went down to Charlotte, North Carolina to meet with Jeffrey Gitomer. That happened toward the end of 2005.

A couple months later, Mike was launching Butterfly Marketing. At the time, we weren't working together. We just kept each other up to speed on each of our businesses. At the time, I was President of a company with Jim Kelly, the Hall of Fame quarterback from the Buffalo Bills. We were putting together some personal development stuff that was going to go online and all sorts of cool stuff.

As things unfolded, that company had pretty much disbanded when Mike had just launched Butterfly Marketing. It was always fun. I still love Jim and everybody who worked hard on that product, but for some reason, it just didn't pick up momentum. It was always exciting. I'd keep him up to date with stuff that was happening with my business, and he'd keep me up to date with his. As mine was kind of dissolving, his was catapulting out of this world.

At the end of January, he launched. The night before it launched, I was the person who was up with him until 3 or 4am, instant messaging him the grammatical changes in the sales letter for Butterfly Marketing. Before we were working together, just as a friend, I said, "I noticed there are some spelling errors. Do you want me to send you over the changes?"

I would instant message him the changes and he would change them on the fly. It worked out pretty well. He did about $1.5 million in sales in one week. Then, after that, I called him and said it was awesome. As people go through big launches, you notice it doesn't end with the big launch. That's actually when it begins, because then the support things happen.

Really, it's a draining period when you go through those launches. Here he was, pretty much on his own. He had a support team that handled the phone calls, emails and stuff like that, but he was the only person in the office at that time.

So we had a good conversation. At the end of that conversation, I heard something in the conversation, and I thought, "Wow." It appeared to be an opportunity for both of us to maximize and use each other's talents to really catapult and take this to the next level.

We had a talk, and next thing you know, he agreed. He said, "Yes, this is the perfect opportunity. What we thought was going to be a multi-million dollar business with what you had going on, Tom, now dissipated where mine has taken off. If we were to team up, it would just continue."

We teamed up. I became VP of Operations with him. So in early February, I moved down to Long Island, and that's pretty much when the explosion happened. We were there pushing each other forward. It's kind of like going to the gym with a partner. It's someone who can help you work out. If you go by yourself, you can always tell yourself, "Oh, I'll do that tomorrow. I'll skip it today. I'm not feeling too good." But if you go with a partner to push you, you exert yourself that extra mile. That's what happened when we were working together.

Next thing you know, we started brainstorming to come out with more stuff. Obviously, the big launch was Butterfly Marketing, and that took a good couple of months, to be honest, getting everything in order for that, but then afterwards, we moved on into more brainstorming to see how we could really help more people in this marketplace achieve the results that they were looking for.

Through that, we continued. That was just one of many launches we did that year, but it turned out very well. I'm continuing into this year and next, and we have some big things in the works right now that are going to really shock. It's going to provide some extreme value, shock people, and point them in the right direction to getting them into online marketing strategy.

It's been a fun journey, and that's the whole thing. We love it so much. It reminds me of riding a bike back in the late 80s. You could do it all day long and never get sick and tired of it, because you love it and you're so passionate about it. Similarly, that's how we feel about this. Nothing is more gratifying.

We travel the world a lot and we go to a lot of seminars. We've had people come up with tears in their eyes and tell us, "Before I heard about you, before I got this product, here were my results. I was darn near bankrupt, tens of thousands of dollars in debt. My marriage was falling apart and everything was crumbling in front of me, but I followed these steps. It can work. Here are the results. I made $40,000 last month. I made $70,000 last month."

They say that with tears in their eyes. They just took action. They had that goal and followed the five steps. Nothing can replace the feeling that that gives. That's why we do what we do. If you look at TheButterflyMarketing.com, TheButterflyMarketingManuscript.com, 2007FigureBusiness.com and The7FigureCode.com, you'll see tons of testimonials.

They aren't the testimonials you see that say, "Hey, I've heard of this new product. I checked it out for a minute and it's great." These are the testimonials of people whose lives were changed. They applied the information we were sharing, and they took massive action.

By all means, we can't take credit for their success, but it definitely was based on the fact that we pointed them in the right direction, showed them the techniques and strategies to follow, but they took massive action and got themselves to accomplish their dreams.

A MIRACLE RECOVERY

— *"A positive attitude has pulled me through the most difficult times."*

Stanley: During your life, you were able to stay positive. What is the importance of staying positive? How can one maintain a positive attitude?

Tom: I'll share something that I haven't shared in all the interviews that I've done, but I feel may answer this question. In 1998, I was in a car wreck. I was in a car that rolled four times; I was ejected from the sunroof. A helicopter lifted me to an airport and I had a near-death experience.

I know there are experiences on TV where you've seen the people with the bright lights and stuff like that. There I was in the field, lying there. The next thing you know, I see someone lying in the field, and I'm confused. I wondered, "Who is that?" I looked, since I'm in the air, and it's me. I see me lying in the field.

As soon as I recognized that it was me, there were bright lights all around, and I was standing there confused, wondering what's going on. Someone comes up beside me and puts their arm around me and instantly, I had no more fear. I knew everything was going to be all right.

We turned 180 degrees around and now, even though it's all bright white light, we're walking towards this huge door, and this bright white light emitting from this door. We start walking towards it and I stopped half way there. I said, "This isn't how it's supposed to end. I know you had more for me to accomplish. Send me back." Immediately, I woke up in the intensive care unit, with a respirator breathing for me.

To make a long story short, I had to learn to walk and talk again, and I actually checked myself out of the hospital against the doctor's orders because they were pretty much preparing me, saying I may never walk or talk the way that I used to. There was no guarantee that I would ever walk or talk normally again. I didn't want to hear that, so I signed all these release forms and checked myself out of the hospital.

I had to use a walker to learn to walk again. It was some period of time before I could talk again, but one of the things that I learned from that experience, and that I have faith and confidence in, is that none of us will be here a second longer or a second shorter than we're supposed to be here.

My mother just passed away two weeks ago and I feel fortunate. I was overseas and got back just in time to spend a couple of days with her before her passing, and that was precious time. I know she's in a better place and out of pain. She accomplished so much in the 52 years while she was here.

Today, I could get run over by something in the parking lot here and this could be my last day. I don't know but I can't worry about that. All I know is that I can sit, talk or stretch, but that will lead me to the goals and directions I have in my life, personally and professionally. None of us can control when that time is.

There will be a time when we each will have a last breath and we each will have our last day. The thing about that is that we don't know when that is. It could be today, next year, 20 years or 50 years from now. None of us know. That's not for us to worry about. It's for us to live passionately, to live not saying, "I would have, should have and could have done this, but I never did."

Take the actions. Be clear. What do you want to be, do and have in this life? Make a list. Anything you could be, do or have, what are they? What type of action steps could you take today to start accomplishing this? Going back to how important a positive attitude is, I feel it is extremely important. A positive attitude has pulled me through the most difficult times.

I guess you could even translate that into faith, having faith that the law of cause and effect isn't going to be wasted. All the time, energy and effort of reading the books, attending the seminars, and taking those steps may not seem to have brought you much further from where you were, but the seeds and the roots are growing, hidden deep in the soil, getting ready to stabilize you when you break the soil.

Once you get those roots established, you will have the self-confidence that when you speak, you know what you're talking about and you're the expert in your field. No matter what occurs, they're not going to shake you. You know what's right and what's not right because you've planted those roots, studied and taken actions. Those actions can produce certain results.

You know if you do X, Y will happen. You have that confidence and belief, the positive attitude and the faith that comes along with that, knowing that your time and effort aren't wasted. Yes, you will have people ridiculing you. I did. Many successful people have faced tremendous ridicule because you're going against the grain.

You're not working the nine-to-five. When I was planting the roots and before I broke ground and started having the results, it was not an easy task. I almost lost my wife over it. I had family ridiculing me, "All you are is a dreamer. Why don't you get real? Why don't you get a real job?" You're going to have ridicule, but you have to know that your efforts are not going to be wasted.

You just have to make that commitment. My first coach, Mike Litman said, "You're either persistent or non-existent." If you go to the gym once this year, you can't expect to be in physically fit shape. If you just read one sentence in a book, you can't expect to get the knowledge that you're supposed to get from that book. It takes a commitment and it takes persistence.

When you're doing those steps, a positive attitude comes hand-in-hand with it. People have worry, negativity or fear when they're not prepared. When you're prepared, nothing can shake you. Obstacles will come. Storms will come and try to push you off path, but you know your destination. You know that you've weathered bigger storms and you know that you will weather this one, too.

It's a "this, too, shall pass" mentality. Positive attitude is a key, as are positive expectations. I'll even add to that. It is important to expect miracles and expect things to work out in your niche. It's like a conspiracy, but a conspiracy where all the pieces are coming together so that you can reach the goals that you have, if you're taking the proper actions, if you have the proper attitude and you have the proper guidance from the mentors that you choose. That's my take on positive attitude.

FINAL WORDS OF WISDOM

— *"It's not about being the self-made millionaire. It's about assembling the proper team to help you accomplish the goal that you have"*

Stanley: We're approaching the end of the call, and I want to end by asking you, if you could start all over again, what three things would you do differently?

Tom: What three things would I do differently?

1. **Get rid of the self-made millionaire mentality** much quicker than I originally did. In leading and setting up the personal development arena, somewhere along the line, I picked up the fallacy of the self-made millionaire. I say fallacy, because all my millionaire friends – and I have a lot of them who are in this bookstore on the bookshelves – have a team.

   It's not about being the self-made millionaire. It's about assembling the proper team to help you accomplish the goal that you have. I tried. I had the mentality that if it's going to be, it's up to me. That probably stole a decade of me trying to doing it all myself, and getting no results, working 20 hours a day, and wondering why my results weren't coming.

   You work yourself to death and you don't get any results. At this time, family and friends are ridiculing you, saying, "You put all this time and effort in and you're not getting any results. You need to not waste your time." If I would have realized at an earlier point, the power of not trying to do it all myself, the power of assembling the proper team to get done what I know needs to be done, in a better, more efficient and much more quick manner, that's the power. That's what I would have loved to have done differently.

2. **Get to a mentor right away.** I had that whole mentality that I can learn it all myself. I'll just read the books. Guess what? You can do that, but it takes a lot more time and the learning curve is much longer than if you just invest in a mentor.

   With that investment, they can pull you through that learning curve. They can say, "Here's what you're doing. I did that, too. Don't do that. Try this." That will save you a year, two years and sometimes even five years' worth of trial and error, and you can get through. It costs a little more up front, but if you're serious about reaching that goal, get a mentor right away.

3. **Lead a four-hour work week** like Tim Ferriss, which is brand new. I met Tim at Stephen Pierce's house a couple of months ago, and it goes back to a saying I heard from a coach I had in 2002. He used to say, "Tom, anybody can achieve great results in 80 hours a week. It doesn't take a superstar to get results in 80 hours a week. The question I pose to you is, Tom, can you get those same results in 20 hours a week? That's a superstar."

Going beyond that is Tim Ferriss is saying about a four-hour work week. He does a lot of outsourcing and stuff like that. The goal wouldn't be to be a total workaholic, but to work smarter, not harder. That's the answer to that question, because I feel the power of your questions will determine where you're going and where you will be.

If you ask yourself, "I'm doing all this in 60 hours or 80 hours a week. How can I get the same results, or maybe even double the results, while getting double the time off?" Those are the questions I would pose to myself much earlier in the process as well. How can I double the results and have double the time off?

If you ask the right questions, you can get the right answers. Ask and you shall receive. If I had to start all over again, those are three things that I would write down right from the outset.

Stanley: Tom, I want to thank you for your time. Are there any final comments you want to add, or let people know about your websites?

Tom: Sure. I actually have a whole bunch of cool stuff coming out. I had a good talk with Mike a little while ago, and he said, "You've got so much to contribute to the personal development and Internet marketing crowd. When are you putting something out?" I answered, "Mike, to be honest, we've been so busy, I haven't even thought of it or put any time and effort into it." He said, "Well, you might want to start putting something down, because you have too much to contribute."

So, there will be some stuff coming out from me very soon, but right now, you can go to TomBeal.com, and from there, you can go to my blog. You'll see a couple things I've put on there. This will jump into my contributing value to people in the personal development arena, as well as Internet marketing.

I'm looking forward to ending this year, and kicking off 2008 in a superb way with MikeFilsaime.com, and some of the things I'll be contributing to the marketplace on my own as well.

CHAPTER 4

GARY AMBROSE:
Email Marketing Expert

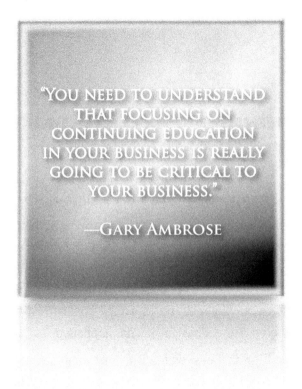

"YOU NEED TO UNDERSTAND THAT FOCUSING ON CONTINUING EDUCATION IN YOUR BUSINESS IS REALLY GOING TO BE CRITICAL TO YOUR BUSINESS."

—GARY AMBROSE

THEY SAY "THE MONEY IS IN THE LIST."

And no other person knows better about list building than Gary Ambrose. Truly a rare-breed, Gary is one of the Internet marketing field's most respected experts in list building, email marketing and email delivery.

71

Coming from a technical background, Gary started online back in 1998 offering online advertising. Not so long later, he created and launched a script that helped list owners to generate a stunning 98 percent opt-in rate, and stayed on number-one Clickbank for months and months.

To date, Gary has released several software programs and created numerous membership sites, with over 125,000 members in total, including EmailAces.com, TheListMachine.com and many more.

Gary was also one of the pioneers of Mike Filsaime's revolutionary Butterfly Marketing and later on became the number-one super affiliate for his million-dollar launch.

And it all began in a car stereo shop in a small town on an island in the Florida Keys…

FROM CHEAP TEENAGER TO SIX FIGURES MARKETER

— *"I got started with Internet marketing basically because I was a cheap teenager living in a very small town looking to get a discount on a car stereo"*

Stanley: Gary, can you tell us when you first got introduced to the Internet?

Gary: Sure. I got introduced to the Internet probably long before most people got into the Internet marketing space. I actually had a computer in my house since I was three years old. So, I started out very young on the computer before there was the Internet. And I got started with Internet marketing basically because I was a cheap teenager living in a very small town looking to get a discount on a car stereo. Here's basically what happened:

I grew up in the Florida Keys, which is a very small series of islands at the very southern most tip of Florida, in a very, very small town. When I was in high school, like many high school guys, I wanted to have a stereo in my car that was loud and obnoxious and shook the car windows and all that good stuff.

And there was only one guy in the Florida Keys who installed car stereos and he happened to go to the same high school. He was an entrepreneur. They ran a family business – a hotel and a restaurant – and he decided he was going to do the car stereos, because he saw a need down there.

I had some basic web and graphics design knowledge given that I had been playing around on a computer for so long. So basically, I approached him and said, "Look, I will put up a website for you if you will do the work for me on my car. Basically, I will pay for the equipment and you do the work and install everything for me, and I will put up a website for you. How does that sound?" And he said, "OK, that's good."

So while I was working on the website and putting everything together, orders started to come in. There was no online ordering system; there was just a form you could print out and fax in to his front desk at his hotel. They did about $50,000 to $60,000 in sales in the first month – and that was before the website was even completed.

At that point, he actually decided that the business was too big and the margins were too small, so he wasn't interested. But to me that was a definite sign that a lot of money was going to be made on the Internet.

This was around 1993-1994, so that's really where I got my real start by just seeing how much money was really coming in online. It was like, "Wow!" We didn't do any marketing; we didn't do any promotion – we didn't even know what marketing and promotion was. We just put up some images, some prices and away we go. Obviously a lot has changed since then. It is not quite so easy now, but that is where I got my start.

Stanley: What did you do in your early days as an Internet marketer?

Gary: A number of years passed and I went from high school to college, where I met a woman there who eventually ended up becoming my girlfriend and now my wife – her name is Jennifer. When I met her, she was getting a marketing degree at college and I really wasn't sure what I was going to do at that point. I was just sort of coasting along. I've never been somebody who enjoyed school all that much.

She graduated in three years and got her marketing degree and she decided it was time to get a job. So she interviewed for a number of places and, because she had entered the workforce so late (she didn't really make a decision to get a job until a little bit later than normal), a lot of the jobs were taken.

So she ended up getting a pretty bad job. She didn't like it, so she quit after two days. She basically came home to the apartment, where we were both living, while I was still asleep and woke me up at about 10am and said, "I just quit my job. We are going to need to make some money." So basically what happened was this:

She is a big fan of soap operas on television and she gets a lot of those magazines. Since those magazines are specifically tailored to the "stay-at-home mother" type crowd, in the back of those magazines, there were a lot of advertisements for work-at-home type of opportunities.

She didn't look at those ads as a way to make money, but instead looked at it and said, "There are a lot of people paying to advertise here. What we should do is we should put up a website that allows people to advertise for this same audience online." And that was the first website we really put up in the Internet marketing space and it was called CashFromHome.com, which is still in operation today.

Basically, what we did is we offered online advertising. At the time, our only competition was America Online and Yahoo!, in which they had a free classified website. We were the only site trying to do paid advertising. It took us a couple of days to get our first advertiser and, in those first few months, we had already done close to six figures in sales.

But again, that was 1998 and now we are almost 10 years out from then. That really opened our eyes to what was going on online because we started to see a lot of the advertisers and what they were advertising. We started to see that people were building email lists, we started to learn about affiliate programs, and we would notice that some people would come back and advertise multiple times.

FOCUS ON CONTINUING EDUCATION
– *"The biggest obstacle for us was success got in our way"*

Stanley: What initial obstacles did you face and how did you overcome them?

Gary: This may not be the typical obstacle story, because, for me, I had been doing websites and graphic design and that type of thing for a number of years. So I didn't really have any technical issues to overcome. A lot of people don't really understand how to put up a website, create graphics, write scripts, put together an ordering system, and any of that kind of stuff. So for me, that was all really second nature.

The biggest surprise to Jennifer and myself was that either of us had never worked for ourselves before. We didn't really understand what it was to have a business. So we didn't pay much attention to income taxes, balance sheets, or keeping good track of cash flow.

So we missed a lot of opportunities that we probably could have done a little bit better on, because we were just excited about making so much money very quickly. The biggest obstacle for us was success got in our way.

We didn't take the time to continue educating ourselves and looking at things like copywriting and sales processes etc. It wasn't really out there about Internet marketing, but it was out there about marketing in general.

That didn't really happen for another four or five years. If we had done that much earlier on in the process, there would have been a huge difference, not only in how much money we made, but how we approached the business in general.

A great example of that is with our advertising services. A lot of the services that we offered, and still offer today, were limited in the number of available blocks they could offer. For example, we would do newsletter advertising and we would only run 10 advertisements in each newsletter and we would have people come back.

And every now and then, we would have newsletters that weren't full and we never offered an upsell to people – we didn't even know about an upsell. Of course, we had seen it in our everyday lives, you get upsold all the time, but to us it was sort of a foreign concept to apply to our own business.

Now, since we have been doing that, I would never in my life offer a website with a product or service of any kind without an upsell option that is available, because there is just so much extra money that we could have made.

So for us, really, the biggest obstacle was that we didn't understand what we were getting into; we didn't really start treating it as a business. We just sort of got lazy, stepped back, and sort of looked at what was going on in amazement, instead of saying, "Wow, there's still a lot of room for growth."

You need to understand that focusing on continuing education in your business – not just education from a single source, but from as many different sources as possible – is really going to be critical to your business.

When we really first started investing in special reports (at that time they weren't even really considered e-books) or even print books from the store, we were very limited in what we were looking at.

We also really weren't thinking correctly about, "OK, this business is doing a process. How can we use the same process in our business? How can we expand it, modify it, and change it? Because it's obviously successful elsewhere, how can we make this work for us?"

DISCOVERY OF INTERNET MARKETING

– *"The biggest thing that we really got out of [the Internet marketing conference] was starting to brand ourselves as individuals and sort of at the top of the business"*

Stanley: How did you eventually discover those Internet marketing techniques?

Gary: For me, it was sort of lucky. We live in Orlando, Florida, which most people know is the home of Disney World and Mickey Mouse, but it is also the second most popular convention city in the United States after Las Vegas.

There was an Internet marketing conference that was held here in Orlando and it happened to be a free conference.

We went to the conference basically to advertise our own services. We actually printed out a bunch of flyers, and between sessions we would hand them out and put them on people's seats. We were sort of surprised that we were the only people doing this. But on the second day, when we went back, about 50 other people had the same idea and the organizers actually had to tell everybody to stop. It seemed like we started a trend.

Honestly, we weren't expecting to learn anything at all from that conference. We thought, "Man, we are making $150,000, $200,000 a year. We know it all. We are doing good stuff here." Then people got up on stage and started talking about copywriting, conversion rates, upsells, cross-sells, backend sales, and different styles of affiliate programs. And even things that are basic now, like some people call it the product funnel, or the profit funnel, or the marketing funnel.

It sounds so stupid to say this now, but, up until that point, we had all these customers and we didn't even have a specific customer list. We just randomly added these people to other lists and treated them like everybody else. Obviously, that was a big mistake.

Stanley: After the Internet marketing conference, what changes did you make to your business?

Gary: It is hard to even to start into that. It has been very dramatic since that time. Basically up until that time, one of the biggest mistakes that we really made in our business was each individual business was branded under its own business name.

So, there wasn't really any correlation between one business that we operated and another. They were all domain names and we didn't use our own names. We didn't mention any names at all; it was almost corporate, I guess you could say.

To us, that was what seemed like how a business should be operated. That is typically what you think of when you hear from the business. You usually hear from some corporate person. So that is what we really did.

But, at the event, the thing that I really noticed was something called the table rush. Obviously being free, this was an event where speakers were paid based on product sales that they made. After each speaker got off the stage, there was like a mad dash to the back of the room where 10, 20, 50, 100 people were ordering these products for $500 to $1,000 each. We were going, "Oh my goodness, these people just made $50,000 in an hour – unbelievable."

At that point, I had really been behind the keyboard, and I had never really tried to brand myself and make a name for myself, or position myself as an expert, or mention the fact that we had got all these different websites and it's me behind these websites. So the biggest thing that we got out of the seminar was starting to brand ourselves as individuals – sort of at the top of the business.

For example, if you look at the most popular large-scale businesses, you know Steve Jobs of Apple, you know Bill Gates of Microsoft, and you know Jeff Bezos of Amazon. We just weren't doing that at all.

So, I made a conscious decision at that point that I was going to start branding myself as an expert in the field, because we had been doing things for quite a while and we had some level of success. I decided that I am going to be one of those people up on that stage in a few years time. I will be up there and people will be listening to me. That has really shifted a lot of where our business has gone as a result.

FROM "SPAMMER" TO EMAIL MARKETING EXPERT

– *"One of the biggest mistakes that I made was focusing so much on attracting all these freebie seekers to my list as opposed to really focusing on generating paying customers and building proper relationships with people"*

Stanley: You are known as an email marketing expert. How did you first get into email marketing?

Gary: The truth is that, like many people who got started in early email marketing and in the mid 90s – not too many would admit this – I started out as a spammer. That was the way it started in the mid 90s; there were no opt-in lists. You gathered email addresses, you made an offering, and you sent it out to people.

There were a number of different ventures along that path, until it started to become a little bit more regulated and got a little bit more difficult. This was probably around 1998. But what I gained as a benefit there is, I've been pretty technical and still continue to be even now.

It is sort of like math: When you know addition, subtraction, multiplication, and division, those are really the building blocks for everything more advanced, such as geometry, trigonometry, and calculus. You can't know any of those things until you know addition and subtraction. It is impossible. The same applies with email.

So I really had a good understanding how email is delivered, how it gets from point A to point B, and how a lot of that stuff worked. Email marketing really started for us when we put up our first affiliate program. We put up a website that is no longer in operation today. It was called SecretFortune.com.

Usually, what you want to strive to do in any marketing process is you want to eliminate as many steps as you can while still having the process make sense. There were opt-in forms and I wanted to eliminate people having to type in their name and email address, because if I can eliminate that step but still get their name and email address, that would be great.

So I created this little JavaScript code that is still in use in a lot of places today. It was released under the name Opt-In Lightening. If you have ever been to a website and you see a little pop up that looks like an official windows box and it has two buttons that say, "OK" or "Cancel to subscribe," I created that script.

We were getting about a 98 percent to 99 percent opt-in rate, because the wording on the page was unlike anything people had ever seen before, which said something like, "Thanks for coming to this page. Would you like seven free reports on affiliate marketing?" And the choices were "OK" or "Cancel." For many people, the obvious answer was, "Would you like seven free reports?"

"Sure, why not? OK."

What that did in the background was that it composed an email that was sent to our email address, and, just like in an autoresponder, we automatically added that person to our list. Now, since I created that script, Microsoft has changed the way that Outlook works and America Online has changed the way that their email program works. I sort of like to think that I was responsible for that. Of course, there is no proof of that. But we started building opt-in list that way.

THE START OF LIST BUILDING

— *"It is truly focusing on people who are interested in buying and have proved that they are interested in buying by pulling out their credit cards or spending some money with me through PayPal, immediately. Those are the people I target"*

Stanley: After building yourself a list, what did you do next?

Gary: I was focusing, like most people teach you to, and they still teach you to do this now even though I think it is entirely wrong, they teach you to build a list by basically following what I call the normal process.

That normal process is: Write a free report, then drive people to a squeeze page, and promise them more stuff for free. Then when they are on your list, just keep sending them more free stuff.

It just wasn't making a whole lot of sense to me. You hear this magic number of $1 per subscriber per month on your list. That is the number that everybody talks about. If you have 1,000 subscribers, you can make a $1,000 a month; maybe you have 2,000 subscribers, you can make $2,000 a month.

And I wasn't making anywhere near that. I had 10,000, 15,000, 20,000 subscribers, and when I send out a message, I make only a couple of hundred dollars. It was good, but it wasn't this $20,000 a month for 20,000 subscribers that I had been promised. I started wondering what was going on, what was wrong.

Around that time, I really started looking at what was going on in a lot of our other businesses. And we had this customer list on our advertising sites that

I mentioned before. And one of our advertising sites was called WeeklyDeal. com and it was really a site that was exclusively for customers who have purchased from us before.

It is basically where we offer a deal or a package deal of some kind on our advertising services, and each week we would put up a new deal on Monday, and we would send the offer to our customer list. And without fail – and it has probably been about for four years – where each and every single week that deal has sold out. It was only three slots of $150, but that was a consistent $450 a week and it has been that way for four years.

I looked at where our traffic was coming from: We were not listed in the search engines, we have never written an article about it, we don't do any pay-per-click advertising, there were no promotions, and our web server logs showed that we get less than 200 visitors to that website every single month.

So it was like 200 visitors a month – laughable almost – but the customer list was where all this money was being generated and that really said something to me, "We are sending out to this small list of customers, we are driving traffic, and that list has been consistently producing profits for us for years. This is something that I need to look at, at focusing on building lists of customers only, people who are buying products and services, people who are at least willing to spend money."

And that is really where my focus has been for the past few years and really why a lot of people know me now. They sort of see all these great results that I have in affiliate promotions for other people and they think that I have got this list of like 500,000, 600,000 people – it has got to be this ridiculously massive list to generate these numbers of sales. But it is not that my list is overly huge, it is that I have a better quality of list than the average person has.

It is truly focusing on people who are interested in buying and have proved that they are interested in buying by pulling out their credit cards or spending some money with me through PayPal, immediately, because those people are hot, ready, and in what I call the "active buying state." They want to spend right now; they're going to spend their money somewhere. It might be with you, it might be with somebody else, but of course, I would like that to be with me.

So, those are the people I target, and I've been doing that for quite a while. That's really the big catalyst behind what looks like an overnight success to many people. It was really just looking at what's been done for the past 100 or 120 years, or however long it is that direct mail has been in use, and applying that to the online marketing world.

THE CREATION AND PIONEERING
OF BUTTERFLY MARKETING

— *"Butterfly marketing wasn't, unlike most people seemed to believe, an overnight success. It was based on what Mike had been doing for a number of previous years, as well as things that I had given him ideas for"*

Stanley: What was your next product or project?

Gary: I had so many different products and projects. Probably the next significant product that we launched was called The List Machine. It focused on helping the newer Internet marketer build their own list. It was a little bit different from the other list building systems in the marketplace at the time.

A couple of other things led up to The List Machine, but it was the first big-time entrance that we had into the viral marketing arena. I've had a number of other sites that were viral marketing or, as many people like to think of them now as Butterfly Marketing sites. But that was the first grand-scale site that we had put into operation and it's been running now for close to three years.

Stanley: You mentioned Butterfly Marketing. Can you tell us how you first met Mike Filsaime and came up with the idea?

Gary: Sure. I was creating a website called Seminar Aces. The basic premise behind the website was that we were going to be finding smart marketers who aren't out there speaking at seminars, but they're still people you'd like to learn from.

The first person whom I interviewed for that website was Russell Brunson. Many people know Russell Brunson now, who is a very successful guy over the last few years. Russell, Mike and I are lumped together in this group, because we all came on the scene at a similar time.

At the end of the interview with Russell, after the button had been stopped on the recording, I asked him, "Russell, is there anybody that you would recommend that I interview?" He said, "Yeah, I know this guy called Mike Filsaime. We've talked a little bit back and forth and I really think you should get in touch with him."

I got in touch with Mike the next day. We were probably on the phone for three or four hours talking about various marketing ideas and a whole bunch of different stuff. We became friends.

Butterfly Marketing wasn't, unlike most people seemed to believe, an overnight success. It was based on what Mike had been doing for a number of previous years, as well as things that I had given him ideas for, ideas that he had gotten from Mark Joyner, and things that he had spoken to Russell Brunson about. Mike took it to market.

The only reason I'm linked to Mike on that is because I was his number-one affiliate by a huge margin. At the time, I was the top-producing affiliate on any launch that any Internet marketing space that had ever been done. Nobody had ever produced that many sales. I had actually produced double the sales that anybody else had ever produced on a launch at that point.

At one point, I had sold close to one out of every five copies of the course that ended up being sold. That was because I focused on building a list of people specifically for that promotion, using the theory that I just discussed – building a list of customers. I built a list of customers specifically for Mike's Butterfly Marketing promotions, getting customers who would purchase the products related to viral marketing.

And then in the same respect, branding yourself and your own name. In our field, branding your own name and giving a recommendation based on your own name, people were sort of buying access to Mike when they bought his course, but they also wanted to buy access to somebody else – they wanted to feel like they have got somebody else to work with.

So I really positioned myself as an expert in viral marketing, showing off cases studies and websites that I had done in the past. That was really the key to the success of that launch and of that promotion.

Butterfly Marketing is really just an example of viral marketing that Mike put his own unique spin on it, gave it a nice name and a nice package, and put everything together. And there really wasn't much more to it than explaining what he had been doing for the past couple of years.

(You can get Mike Filsaime's Butterfly Marketing at TheButterflyMarketing.com)

A DAY IN THE LIFE OF A "NIGHT OWL"

– *"My day starts after most people's days end. I actually have sort of a ritual that I have been doing for almost 10 years now. What that helps me do is shift my mind from everyday to working time"*

Stanley: Unlike most people, you actually work at night. Why do you do that?

Gary: Well, it started out of necessity, actually. Nowadays, we think of web hosting as being a very inexpensive thing. It's $8 a month, in some cases, or maybe even less. But back then, when I first started web design and programming in the early 90s, web severs were very expensive and you couldn't develop a website on your own computer and you couldn't develop things locally and then deploy them onto a website somewhere else. You had to work in real time on a functioning webserver.

My original business name was Panic Web and it was called that because I would get phone calls from panicked business owners wanting me to fix their websites. I had to work overnight, because that is when the customers were not viewing the site and the site had to be back in operation when the sun came up. So for years, that is how I was doing things.

Now that I am a parent, I have two children and another one on the way, and I work from my home, I don't have any distractions at night. Your children are not going to come in and say, "Hello" at three in the morning; you can't run to the grocery store at three in the morning; you are not going to be getting solicitation calls at three in the morning. All of that kind of stuff is sort of blocked out in the middle of the night. My kids are asleep, so they are not coming in, so none of us feel bad about not feeding them.

So, for me, I sort of got lucky, but I really enjoy it because I am alone in my own little world with no other distractions. There is nothing going on that is going to take away my attention from what I need to get done. It is quiet; it is somewhat solitary, but as I said, it allows me to focus specifically on what it is that I need to be doing.

I know a number of entrepreneurs in the Internet marketing field who have a very similar schedule to what I do. And they may not have that schedule all the time, but when it comes down to finishing a large-scale project or really getting something done, many of the people who I know in this space say that the best work that they get done is really in the middle of the night when nobody else is in the office. It is just them and them alone and they could focus.

Stanley: Can you describe a typical day in your life?

Gary: Sure. Typically for me, I work obviously very late. I usually won't get started working until about 10pm. I will first have dinner; I will watch a couple of television shows; I will give my kids their bath, put them to sleep; I will spend some time with my wife, and then she is about to go to sleep, because she wakes up with them and takes them to school and that kind of stuff.

So, for me, my day starts after most people's days end. I actually have sort of a ritual that I have been doing for almost 10 years now, which is before I start work – I work in my own house, my office is in my house – I leave my house and I go to a convenience store here called 7-Eleven and I get a frozen drink called the Slurpee. I have been doing that every night – it is sort of like my cup of coffee. What that helps me do is shift my mind from everyday to working time.

Most people do that on their morning commute, that's when they make the shift from personal time to work time. For me, it has really been pretty beneficial and I actually can tell a difference in my focus and my ability to get things done when I don't make that trip, because I don't have that shift in my mindset.

I work from about 10pm to 4 or 5am, depending on what I need to get done, and I will be asleep from 5am until 1pm. That is about the time my kids are getting home from school. So when they are home from school, essentially they see me the whole entire time that they are home, which is great.

It is something that I really wanted to make sure that I could get done. One of the main reasons that I started working for myself in the first place was that I really wanted to be able to be here and be around when my kids were home, go to soccer games, and do that kind of stuff. But that is my typical day.

It usually starts when I get working. I will turn on the computer and I will download all of my emails. I will go through my inbox really quickly and if there is anything that needs to be answered, I answer it right then before I get into anything else.

Then I go into my support boxes after my support teams checks everything first and then whatever is left behind that needs an answer from me as the owner of those sites, I will answer those questions. Once those things are done, I really get focused on whatever the project at hand there happens to be.

This evening, I had this interview scheduled, obviously, but before that, I had to speak with a programmer about something that I am having developed. Then I have on my schedule to write some email copy to send out about an affiliate promotion.

Then I worked on some graphics for one of the websites that I am in the process of developing. After this phone call, I am actually going to be sending that email out, because I like to do so a little bit earlier in the mornings and that is really going to end my day.

TO BE SUCCESSFUL, YOU NEED TO BE CONFIDENT

— "You have to be confident... confident bordering on the point of arrogance"

Stanley: In you opinion what mindset and belief should one have to succeed in Internet marketing?

Gary: The most important thing that somebody needs to have if they are going to be successful – not just in Internet marketing, but I believe in any type of entrepreneurial business – is that they need to be confident, almost confident bordering on arrogance. That may sound a bit strange, but I am going to explain it like this:

When I get started on a project, like a lot of the things that I am working on now, in my mind, there is absolutely no question whatsoever that each and every one of those projects is going to be successful. I have no doubts whatsoever. A competitor can come into the field, I could care less. Somebody could undercut my idea, that is perfectly fine. I will be successful. It will happen.

And I sort of think it becomes a self-fulfilling prophecy. What I mean by that is that if you feel that your project is going to be successful, you are going to be more excited about working on it; you are going to put in better effort; you are not going to dread doing it and put in minimal effort.

But, if you're not confident that it's going to be successful from the very beginning, you almost set yourself up to fail right from the start, because you don't put in your best effort; you're not excited about working on it.

You start to cut corners just so that you can get it done. By the time you're finished, you have put in so much less effort, half-hearted effort, that you are almost better off not doing it in the first place, because all you're going to do is cement that in your head that, "OK, well look, I thought I was going to fail and now I failed. Great."

But, for me, it's always that I will be successful. I've had an amazing streak going, and I hope I can continue that streak, which is that I have yet to have a product or service that has not been profitable. In the entire 10 years since I officially started the legal business, every product or service I've offered has been profitable. Many of them have been profitable beyond what I expected they would be. And all of the services that I am working on now, I have no doubt whatsoever that they will be profitable.

You have to be confident, and, like I said, confident bordering on the point of arrogance – almost to the point where if somebody tells you that's not going to work, you say, "Well, you know what? You're wrong. It will work. I'm going to prove it to you. Now watch me do it. And in a year when it is working, then come back and try to tell me."

A great example of a guy from the real, actual business world that everybody knows is Steve Jobs from Apple. If you look at Apple, Steve Jobs is widely considered to be an arrogant, very difficult to work for, extremely opinionated, just a difficult guy to be around. But, he's very, very confident.

Most people thought that the iPod was going to be a joke. Well, obviously, that didn't exactly turn out like the analysts expected. I was reading a five-year-old article just two days ago about how there was no way that Apple Stores would ever be profitable. It was a laughable idea. How could an Apple Store be profitable? Well, right now, Apple Stores are some of the most profitable stores per square foot of any retailer in the United States.

Then, you look at the iPhone. Of course, everybody knows about the iPhone now. How can a company that's never produced a mobile device revolutionize or change anything that has to do with the telecom industry? A phone with no buttons? How ridiculous does that sound? When you think about it on the surface, a phone with no buttons? Yeah, that's going to sell real well *(sarcastic)*. Well, I've got one sitting here on my desk.

Steve Jobs is a great example of somebody who, in the face of all sorts of criticism from the outside world, stuck to his guns – and you can tell – nothing was compromised along the entire process. Everything was done the way that he wanted it, he did not compromise, and the confidence shows through.

DO IT NOW!

– *"The problem is most people want to make a million dollars immediately and they forget that along the way to a million dollars you have to make your first dollar"*

Stanley: Gary, I want to thank you for your time. Do you have any final comments you want to add or let people know about your main website?

Gary: I always do this at the end of a call rather than the beginning, specifically because I only want people to visit this site if they actually listened to what I had to say or read what I had to say and enjoyed what I had to say. A lot of people mention their websites at the beginning, and tell them to go opt in, and do this and that. To me, that doesn't really make any sense.

So I've got a website called GaryTheAce.com. You're not going to find a heck of a lot there right now, but if you enjoyed what I had to say here, I think you are going to enjoy what you see on the other side there.

I guess, basically in closing, the one thing that a lot of people say, "Just take action." It's sort of a trademark and I know people get tired of hearing "just take action." So, although I want to say, just take action, I'm going to say it a little bit differently.

If you've been researching a business, or you've created e-books or products or services of any kind, the odds are that you already have the knowledge you need to make your first few thousand dollars. You don't need to learn any more. You don't need to buy anything else. You don't need to keep searching.

All you need to do is to take the information you already have and start using it. There is this law that basically goes, "Until you've made your first dollar, you're not going to make $100. Until you make $100, you're not going to make $1,000. Until you make $1,000, you're not going to make $10,000. Until you make $10,000, you're not going to make $100,000."

The problem is, most people want to make a million dollars immediately, and they forget that along the way to a million dollars you have to make your first dollar. Just make your first dollar. Do it now because you're not going to make a million dollars until you've made your first.

CHAPTER 5

WILLIE CRAWFORD:
Internet Marketing Pioneer

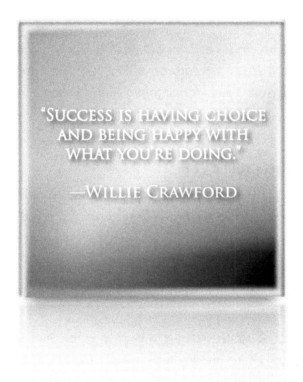

"SUCCESS IS HAVING CHOICE AND BEING HAPPY WITH WHAT YOU'RE DOING."

—WILLIE CRAWFORD

WILLIE CRAWFORD IS TRULY ONE OF THE PIONEERS IN INTERNET *marketing and a classic rags-to-riches story.*

Growing up on welfare on a small tobacco farm in North Carolina, Willie endured many tough obstacles as a young child, including both mental and cultural limitations.

No telephone... no television... exposed to all kinds of poisons... 14 years old before he ever went to a movie theater... 16 years old before he ever tasted steak...

Most of the people he knew were on welfare, including his grandmother who raised him. Without success models and mentors to learn from, it wasn't until many years later that he discovered the secrets that everyday life teaches us.

Yet, despite of all the hardships, he made it through college and a military career. Then towards the end of his military career, Willie decided to pursue his dream and started his own online business.

He began his online career building niche sites and still makes six figures per year with his first cooking niche site alone.

Today, Willie Crawford is a multi-million dollar success and operates over 200 active websites. He is a published author, seminar host, internationally featured speaker, business mentor and joint venture broker.

GROWING UP ON WELFARE

— *"My parents separated when I was very young and my grandmother ended up taking care of me and my two younger brothers, so we lived on her to-bacco farm"*

Stanley: I understand that you actually grew up on welfare during your childhood. Let's just start off from there. Tell us a bit about that and how you managed to overcome that.

Willie: My parents separated when I was very young and my grandmother ended up taking care of me and my two younger brothers, so we lived on her tobacco farm. She was already 65 years old and I was about five years old, so she was an old lady taking care of three children and needed to have government assistance in order to be able to afford to feed and clothe us.

That's how we ended up in that situation. As I went through high school, I did very well in school, so my teachers noticed how I smart I was, and they encouraged me to apply for college, and that was what exposed me to a lot of things outside of that poverty lifestyle on the farm.

I went to North Carolina State University. When I was growing up, I didn't really visit a lot of universities, because most people that lived near where I live didn't go to college. They were too poor to even think about it. So I had only visited one university when I was in school, and it was at the local carnival state fair, and it was the only university I was familiar with. I applied there and they accepted me.

Stanley: How was university back then? How did it eventually lead you to the military?

Willie: It was challenging, because I didn't take the right pre-college or college prep courses in high school. The school teachers would look at children, and they would, I guess in their mind, decide whether or not they felt that you're going to continue with college, so you could immediately begin with college and they would encourage you to take the classes that prepared you for college.

But if you were in that group of kids that were too poor and didn't get to pick what college, they wouldn't encourage you to pick classes. So when I arrived at college, I wasn't so prepared. It required a lot of work on my part. I earned good grades, I made the Dean's list many times and I did well. But it was a lot of work, because I didn't have the preparation and the background for it.

Then after my third year of college, I noticed RO23, the jet rocket training course. It had lots of students walking down the campus in uniform, and you could pick classes for the RO23 military program, and they were easy classes, where you could easily get good grades with those, but at the same time it was a recruiting tool for the military, and that's how I was exposed to the air force.

I wasn't sure what I wanted to do after college, so I decided to try the military course, what I thought would be short term, but I ended up making a full career out of it. I flew inside military airplanes, and I traveled to about 47 different countries and explored the world, so it was a lot of fun.

GOING ONLINE

— *"I need to start my own business, but because I was moving around so often with the military, I needed something that was portable, I needed a job that I could be doing no matter where I was"*

Stanley: How did you get started online while you were in the military?

Willie: I think my job in the military was actually a good job. It paid well. I took business and economics while I was in college, and I always wanted my own business. So, after about 14 years in the military, I was thinking about leaving, because I just saw myself not making as much progress as fast as I wanted to.

I thought, "Well, I need to start my own business." But because I was moving around so often with the military, I needed something that was portable; I needed a job that I could be doing no matter where I was. And that's what caused me to notice the Internet. Looking at what I was doing, I was in an office job for the military at that time, and there we had access to the Internet, and this was late 1995.

So I started looking around on the Internet and noticed that there were advertisements telling you that you could make money on the Internet, like a lot of these magazines that will tell you that you can make money selling different things, and different home-based businesses. So I just started looking around on the Internet in late 1995, and then in 1996, I decided that I was going to give that a try.

Stanley: What did you do in your early days as an Internet marketer?

Willie: I went online and noticed that there were lots of people offering free newsletters – not as many as today of course – but there were some free newsletters out there. So I subscribed to just about every one that I could find, and I printed the e-zines out, and then I hoped that I would be out flying around the Pacific Ocean.

I was a navigator. The navigator basically plans the flight and keeps track of where the airplane is going. Once you're away from land, you just point the airplane in the direction that you're going. It's not a lot of work to keep going; you're not going to fly into a mountain or anything. Just every hour, it's my job to confirm where the airplane is, and to make sure that it's burning fuel at the proper rate, so it doesn't run out before it gets to its destination, things like that.

This meant I had a lot of free time in the airplane, and I used that time to read the e-zines that I printed out. That's when I first started studying Internet marketing, just subscribing to every newsletter I could find and joining discussion lists. They had a lot of email discussion lists back then, where people could basically discuss business ideas.

FIRST MAJOR SUCCESS
— *"Give them what they tell you they want to buy"*

Stanley: What happened next? What was your first project?

Willie: I decided to go ahead and build a website, and my first two websites were on free host. They were on FreeYellow.com and AngelFire.com where they give you free web space. I don't remember how much disk space there was, but it wasn't a lot. You use a template and you build a website that has a domain name, probably like AngelFire.com/SomeOtherWord. So I built very ugly websites.

I then found the very early versions of affiliate programs, which enabled you to sell maybe telephones, calling plans, and different things. So I signed up for a number of these, and I also signed up to retail some of the early Internet marketing books and courses.

As I did, I joined a number of discussion lists, and on those lists, as I'm reading and also posting to the list, I was using a Hotmail email address and my FreeYellow account. I had people who had directly emailed me back and said, "If you're serious about building a business, first of all, you need your own domain name and you need to stop using that Hotmail account, because only people who are hiding something use those throw away email addresses. If you're not confident enough in your own business abilities to invest in a domain name, then nobody is going to take you seriously." So I had people who cared enough out there, to advise me to develop a more professional appearance.

Then I kept reading that you need to find a niche, that you need to not sell everything under the sun, but instead to find some group of people that you could connect with and find a passion. I built one site at WillieCrawford.com, which was all about Internet marketing. It was my typical Internet marketing site, where I sold affiliate products.

It did OK, but my second site was when I said, "Well, I know how to cook the food I grew up with on the farm." I built a site and all I did was post 15 recipes that I learned while I was a child in forums, and I appropriated the mailing lists in order to keep the sites from looking ridiculous. So I put up a form that said, "Hey, subscribe to my list and I'll send you free recipes."

I was supposed to do the form, so I built the form using the Matt Light's Free Script, and all of a sudden people were visiting my site, exchanging recipes, and were discussing recipes on the site, as well as subscribing to my lists.

Shortly thereafter, they emailed me and said, "Do you have a cookbook?" The reason they asked that was because they enjoyed the recipes so much that it was a pleasant experience for them every day to look forward to getting their recipes. When they got them, they assumed that it had come from my domain and that I must have that recipe.

So they asked about a cookbook and I said, "No, but I'm thinking about writing one." They said, "Well, we'll buy it if you do write one." "OK I'm taking down your order." I set up the order form and I had over 100 orders before I wrote the first page of my cookbook.

I learned actually that many information marketers announce that the product is available before it's ready. What that does is it forces you not to procrastinate. When you have people already ordering a product, you have to get it done, or refund the money.

So I sat down and, using Microsoft Word, I made a list of recipes that were appropriate for a country cooking cookbook, and the recipes that I had, I just typed up, and the ones I didn't have, but I thought should be in the book, I'd jot down and then test it. So I wrote a cookbook. It still sells extremely well to this day. In fact, between now (October 2007) and New Year's Day, I hope to make probably $250,000 in sales of that cookbook.

But that's unusual, because the thing is that for that particular product, most of my sales are made in the holiday season, as in the U.S. holidays. When Thanksgiving approaches, people are looking for recipes to impress, and then they have Christmas, where people are looking for Christmas recipes and Christmas presents. Then New Year's Day comes up, and again, they're looking for traditional recipes to impress relatives.

So, in that timeframe, I'll have days where there will be 50,000 people visiting my website – very few days – because they're looking for recipes. They're online, and it's approaching time to finish their Christmas shopping, they'll order 20 copies of my cookbook as presents and stocking stuffers. So, it's an unusual situation, but it's a very concentrated period of a lot of sales.

Stanley: What do you think was the biggest reason behind the huge success of your cookbook?

Willie: The biggest reason behind the success of the cookbook was that I gave people what they wanted. On that site, I had a sign-up form for people to subscribe and exchange recipes, and I said "OK, now I'm emailing these people every day a list of recipes, I need to sell them something."

So I looked for products to sell them, and I tried to sell them medicines for diabetics that are home delivered, telephone calling plans, and Internet marketing products, but that wasn't what they were interested in. They were interested in learning to cook better and exchanging recipes, so when I offered them the cookbook, they all started buying.

Every time I offered a different cookbook to that list, they purchased. When I offered other products, they didn't buy. What does that tells you is that you give them what they tell you they want to buy.

Stanley: What's the URL of that site?

Willie: The URL of that site is Chitterlings.com, because that's the name for a dish for pig intestines. It's a popular dish in Southern United States.

It's one of those things, that, if you've ever been in a house where chitterlings appear in a dish, because they have such a strong odor, you'll remember. That's why I chose the name, because I knew that the name would be easy for my customers to remember.

In fact, I had meat packaging houses and safe companies offer me up to $300,000 to purchase that domain name. It's valuable now, just the domain name itself. Of course, like I said, I have days where I get 25,000 to 50,000 visitors to my website, just looking for food and recipes. So it has a true value now.

SEMINAR SUCCESS

— *"If I could put on a seminar and have 50 people attend, paying me $1,000 each, that's $50,000!"*

Stanley: What was your next project after that?

Willie: I was doing quite well in the cooking niche. I started talking about why some of the things I did worked properly, so my next project was actually into speaking at Internet marketing seminars. Dr. Bob Silber was organizing a seminar at the time and he noticed me when I was posting on Tony Blake's discussion forum.

So I was asked by Bob Silber to speak at his seminar. All the speakers at that seminar gained the rights to market the videos from the seminar, so that was my next product that I had to do.

At that seminar, I met a lot of people, and agreed to do other projects with certain people. I met Marty Foley there, who is excellent in PPC search engines, so Marty and I agreed to do two teleseminars on how to use PPC, and we called it Mastering the Pay-Per-Click. It did well and we sold that product for a long time, but it's out of date now. I met several other people at that seminar that I did projects with.

Stanley: In 2003, you hosted your first workshop. Tell us a bit about that.

Willie: I attended Bob Silber's seminar in December 2002, and that was actually the first seminar I had ever attended, and Bob invited me to speak, so that was unusual. I looked at how big this is set up, and I said to myself, "Well, this is a great way to make money. If I could put on a seminar and have 50 people attend, paying me $1,000 each, that's $50,000!"

What about my expenses? I didn't know at the time. So I was thinking to myself that I wanted to host a seminar, and I announced to my friends and everybody that I knew. I scheduled the seminar for that April and I started timing it. And within four months of ever attending a seminar, I actually hosted my first live seminar.

Stanley: How was the seminar?

Willie: We didn't have the number of attendees that I had hoped for. The reason was that the vast majority of seats sold at a seminar are sold by the seminar promoter. If you see a seminar that has 10 speakers, and they're all well-known names, and they are speaking maybe two or three times a month at different seminars, those people don't have the time, they can't promote the seminar that much because they have to work on it to promote.

They can't just keeping sending their lists email after email about seminars. So they all did very little promoting, so inviting them and thinking that the seminar was going to be a success was not the case. I had to do most of the promoting myself, but I can say that the seminar was a success.

I noticed Stephen Pierce online back then from reading his book TheWholeTruth.com. I gave Stephen a call to see if he'd be interested in speaking at my seminar. Steven had never spoken at an Internet marketing seminar back then, and my seminar was the first one he spoke at.

He sold quite a few seats for me because his book *The Whole Truth* was doing about $60,000 per month on ClickBank. He had a lot of very well-known friends, so I had a good turn out. Stephen was very good friends with John Reese, so when John found out that Stephen was speaking, John showed up. Armand Morin was also there, along with a lot of fairly well-known people, but the seminar itself was small.

What the seminar did was it still set me apart from many others in the Internet marketing world, because so many people think about hosting a seminar, but many of them don't go through with it or they haven't sold as many tickets as they hoped for, so they cancel it. So, that's what set me apart from the rest in the world of Internet marketing.

THE INTERNET MARKETING INNER CIRCLE
— *"It's a real community where people actually work together"*

Stanley: After your sort of mini-success with your seminar, what was your next project?

Willie: My next project was a series of mostly e-books. I'm a very prolific writer. When I first came online, I meet Jim Daniels and he published a newsletter that I really liked, and I bought a book he wrote.

I liked his writing style so much that, when I started publishing a newsletter, I used the same tone that he used, which was basically to write as if you're sitting across the table, giving advice to maybe a nephew or something, or one of your children. I started writing in that style and my readers instantly connected with me.

Then I just wrote a series of e-books on different topics, none of which were huge successes. But they all did OK. What happened at that point was that I started building a list and selling affiliate products. And at the same time, I decided that I wanted to help more people who were struggling to find affiliate products and launch their own products.

So I decided to create a membership site of my own. That was two years ago, but it never really took off in the first year. The site is at TheInternetMarketingInnerCircle.com. I looked at all these big name marketers with huge lists, and I knew that most people, when they get ready to launch a product, they want these people to help them promote their product, but it's not possible for them to help everyone.

So I put together a site to help people to build their own networks, build their own group of people who can help them launch a product and promote a product. That's my flagship product; that's my baby right now.

Stanley: How many sales did you actually generate with that?

Willie: The membership itself is less than 1,000 right now, but a membership itself costs $497 at the same time. It's not one of those sites designed to be like a typical Internet marketing launch, where everybody email their list at one time, and next week people have forgotten about it. I want this site to be around five years from now, 10 years from now, and I want it to be active. So it's a real community where people actually work together.

For example, in the middle of September 2007, I posted this project on the private membership forum the site has. I said, "I want to write a book that teaches people how to actually make money online. Most people would be pretty happy if they just made $100 per day if all it took was one hour a day or two hours a day doing that. Many of us know how to do that because we do it all the time. $100 per day is $3,000 per month and many people would be happy with that."

The members inside my membership site at The Internet Marketing Inner Circle, said, "Yeah, let's do that!" About 30 people said they could write chapters. I wanted to do it fairly quickly and that cost all of us about 22 job hours. We wrote an e-book and called it *20 Ways to Make $100 Per Day Online,* and that e-book launched on October 8, 2007. You can get a copy of the e-book over at 20ways100dollars.com.

In the first week of launch, that e-book made about $35,000 in sales and it's only a $27 e-book. We used the $7 Script by Jonathan Leger, where when a person buys the e-book, they can turn around and resell it and get 100 percent commission. But it doesn't mention that anywhere on the sales letter. We don't want that to be the reason they buy the book. We don't want them to buy the book just because they know they can make money by selling it.

So, after they buy the book, then they see on the download page that there's an affiliate program that pays them 100 percent commission. Many people who bought the book in the last week have turned around and made $3,000 to $4,000 just selling the e-book itself.

That's probably our most successful product as a group. The membership in the membership site is not intended to be huge. I would like maybe about 5,000 members who all work together. We can't work together on every project, but we can do a lot of projects together.

SUCCESS IS HAVING CHOICE

— *"So many people do jobs because they need the money; they don't do them because they enjoy doing them"*

Stanley: What do you define as success? Do you think you have achieved that kind of success?

Willie: I think I have achieved success. To me, success is probably above all things being happy with what you're doing. It is having a choice in what I do. So many people do jobs they do not want to do. They get up and they go to work at jobs they hate, and they do it because they have to. The work I do, I do it because I want to, and I do it when I want to, and where I want to.

My typical day, if I wanted it to be, would be to get up and take my laptop with my wireless Internet card, and go sit on the beach all day. If I want to do that, I can. I can run my business from the beach, because of wireless Internet and satellites and things like that. So to me, it's about having choice.

A part of that comes from when I was in the military. Soldiers get told what to do. You have some choice, but mostly you were given orders, and although it was a military career, I learned not to like being told but I like having choice.

For me, success is having choice, and it's also being happy with what you're doing. So many people do jobs because they need the money; they don't do them because they enjoy doing them.

Stanley: Willie, I want to thank you for your time. Do you have any final comments you want to add, or let people know about your website where they can get more information about you?

Willie: The best way to get more information about me is at WillieCrawford. com/Blog. That's where I post my thoughts about Internet marketing, and where I teach a lot of things and I know and automate my day-to-day experience.

CHAPTER 6

MICHEL FORTIN:
Online Copywriting Expert

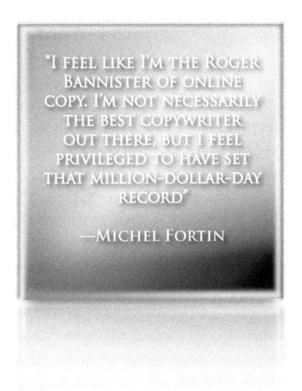

"I FEEL LIKE I'M THE ROGER BANNISTER OF ONLINE COPY. I'M NOT NECESSARILY THE BEST COPYWRITER OUT THERE, BUT I FEEL PRIVILEGED TO HAVE SET THAT MILLION-DOLLAR-DAY RECORD"

—MICHEL FORTIN

MICHEL FORTIN WAS ANYTHING BUT NORMAL, AND BY ALL *accounts, an unlikely candidate for becoming a copywriter, let alone a top-selling copywriter.*

Born with severely deformed legs, abused by his alcoholic father who could not accept the fact that he was a failure, Michel grew up with an immense fear of rejection and became almost an agoraphobic by staying in his bedroom throughout his entire teen.

Trying to fight off his fear of rejection, he dived into the world of sales. But his lack of sales forced him to declare bankruptcy at only 21 years old.

Severely in debt... living off instant noodles from Chinatown just to survive... things hit rock bottom for Michel.

Then he discovered the key. He turned his life around.

Now 20 years later, Michel Fortin has become one of the world's top online copywriting experts. He has an uncanny knack for writing persuasively and knows how to use words to "grab readers by the eyeballs", boost response to record rates, and transform floundering businesses into mega-moneymaking machines.

His track record speaks for itself.

In the past few years alone, he was instrumental in selling hundreds of millions of dollars worth of products and services for a wide variety of clients, stretching across hundreds of different and unrelated industries.

The famous sales letter he wrote for John Reese's Traffic Secrets sold a record-breaking $1.08 million online in under 24 hours. A few weeks later, another sales letter for a completely different product generated over $1.04 million in three weeks.

The chances are, even if you have never once visited his sites, you will have read some of his copy on other people's sites.

His client roster reads like a who's who of Internet marketing: John Reese, Yanik Silver, Frank Kern, Stephen Pierce, Jay Abraham, Corey Rudl, Armand Morin, David Garfinkel, Mark Joyner, Simon Grabowski, Shawn Casey, Ryan Deiss, Craig Perrine and many more...

For Michel, he has achieved success.

FROM A STARVING FAILURE TO THE SUCCESS DOCTOR

— *"Do what you fear and the death of that fear is certain" (Henry David Tho-*
   reau)

Stanley: Let's take you way back and start off with your childhood. I understand that you actually grew up enduring many difficulties. Tell us a bit about
your childhood and how you eventually overcame that.

Michel: To make a long story short, I was born with severely deformed legs
and feet. I wouldn't say that severe but they were severe to a child. In fact, they
grew inward and that was because of the fact that I was a pretty huge baby
growing inside a very tiny womb. My mother is only four-and-a-half-feet tall
and I was born at 12 pounds.

Because I was deformed in that way, my father, who could not accept the
fact that he failed, became an alcoholic and labeled me as a failure and was very
emotionally abusive with me. As I grew up, I had this immense fear of rejection. I was somewhat of an agoraphobic. I pretty much lived my entire childhood and my early teen years inside my bedroom for a variety of reasons.

One was because I hated going out. I hated meeting people. I feared rejection immensely. Second, it was just to stay away from my father, who was
pretty much drunk all the time. In fact, my father is now institutionalized with
a disease called Korsakov's syndrome, which is a mental illness brought on by
years of alcohol abuse.

Nevertheless, this immense fear of rejection caused me not to want to meet
new people and it was a struggle. In my late teen years, I wanted to fight those
fears. There's a very famous quote by a philosopher by the name of Henry David
Thoreau, who said, "Do what you fear and the death of that fear is certain."

I thought, "OK, I have to do what I fear. That means I have to go out there
and be rejected." How can you do that? That's why when I was very young, I
decided to dive into the world of sales and selling. I decided to do that because
I felt, "What better way is there to fight the fear of rejection, when you're in an
industry where you're rejected constantly?"

In salesmanship and the industry of sales, especially when you go door-to-door, you get the door slammed in your face all the time. That was the beginning. In fact, I was living on strict commissions. Because of the fact that I feared rejection, actually, I had no income to show for it.

I was living on credit cards for many months – almost a year. I put myself in enormous debt just to survive, because I really wanted to fight these fears of rejection. In fact, I was 21 years old when I first declared bankruptcy.

Then I realized something that was kind of cool. I asked myself, "What can I do in order to fight this fear?" I could still continue to fight the fear of rejection, but rather than trying to go out there and prospect for people who at least would listen to my sales pitch and my sales presentation, I could write copy. I could write lead-generation sales letters where I could actually get people to call me to book an appointment with me.

I started to do that and I literally became the number-one salesperson for a Fortune 500 company here in Canada for about eight months running. I realized that there has to be something to this copywriting thing. That's what helped me to dive into the world of copywriting because I realized I no longer had to be rejected.

Of course, a lot of it was also about positioning. I'm a big fan of positioning versus prospecting. That's where my start in copywriting really flourished, because I no longer had to be rejected in sales; I no longer had to go out there and prospect for new clients. I could simply write lead-generation sales letters and I would just have a very few people, who were highly targeted and interested in hearing my sales presentation, to call me.

Now, whether they say, "Yes" or "No" that's all about selling, that's at the sales presentation. From the prospecting perspective, I was no longer rejected and that's my story.

Stanley: Tell us about your early days as a copywriter.

Michel: When I started out, I wasn't really a copywriter. I was using copywriting. Please understand that I was not a copywriter. I was always in sales. What happened was that eventually I decided to become a marketing consultant.

In fact, I dove into an area that I was usually employed in, which was cosmetic surgery. I was a marketing consultant for doctors of cosmetic surgery. In fact, that's why I call my company The Success Doctor, because I helped doctors become successful.

Again, I wasn't really considering myself as a copywriter. I was a marketing consultant. I wrote all the copy for their newsletters, direct-mail packages, infomercials etc. I was also training their sales people on how to consult patients before they actually see the doctor.

One thing led to another, where I was hired more and more by people who wanted to hire me for my copywriting services and they weren't just cosmetic surgeons. I started to consult with lawyers, accountants etc. I was primarily in the service industry. Then I worked in used-car sales, vacuum sales, and musical instrument sales. I decided to completely focus on copywriting only and that's when I really became a copywriter, so to speak.

FROM OFFLINE TO ONLINE

— *"A good yellow page ad asks for action and that's what we call direct response"*

Stanley: What happened next?

Michel: Whenever I decided to go into copywriting, one thing I did in the process – this was actually happening at the same time; it didn't really happen before – as a "marketing consultant" was to help increase the exposure and the visibility of my clients who were doctors. This was in the early 1990s.

One new area that just started out, to me, was this digital form of yellow pages. I was a big fan of yellow page advertising and when I saw this thing called the Internet, I said to myself, "Wow! We can actually go online, register a domain name, and literally have your yellow page ad on the Internet."

It was a backup, because if people ever want to look up cosmetic surgery or any of my clients' services or businesses, they could simply look it up in the yellow pages or they could just go online.

The Internet wasn't big in those days, but I was a big fan of multiplying your exposure of being prolific in being as many places as possible. My main philosophy is to position yourself as an expert. Once you position yourself, people want to do business with you.

The next step is to find you. So when people decide they want to do business with you – when you have a catchy tagline, company name, product name, or service that people remember, that people believe in and they want to know more about you – they'll look you up.

You need to be in as many places as possible. What I was doing as part of my consulting practice was to design websites for my doctor clients. And I said to myself, "I better start doing the same thing I've been teaching all my doctor clients to do, so I might as well have my own website too." That's when I registered SuccessDoctor.com.

At first, that website was just like a yellow page ad. It was just meant to be a backup. It was just meant to be a brochure of sorts. So if people were to ever look up my name – if they heard my name offline, if they ever went online – they could find out how to contact me. That's what my concept of the Internet was at that time.

What happened, slowly but surely, was that I decided to use the Internet like a good yellow page ad. A good yellow page ad, of course, is not an ad where you just say, "Here's my name, here's what I do, here's my number." A good yellow page ad asks for action and that's what we call direct response.

What I did was I wrote a small booklet that was actually my sales letter. It was actually in the form of a booklet called The Ten Commandments of Power Positioning. I've used that booklet to sell my services. I would give this booklet away for free to a lot of doctors and that would get me a lot of jobs, a lot of work, a lot of projects, and a lot of clients.

I decided to digitize that book and deliver that book online on my website. When people would visit my website, they would have the ability to download that book. In fact, early in my career, when a lot of people weren't doing this, I decided to offer the book only if you subscribed to my list, so I started creating an email list.

I wrote a newsletter called *The Profit Pill* in those days. My website started to distribute that book and it took off – it exploded. My website then became one of the top websites. I became known as one of the top copywriters online. I was hired by a lot of the top marketers to write copy for them: Shawn Casey, Frank Kern, Armand Morin, Kirt Christensen, Stephen Pierce, Yanik Silver etc. That's when my business really exploded.

Later on, I literally transformed my website into a sales machine where people can actually ask for quote requests, where I have a portfolio, and so on and so forth. That's just my flagship side.

THE POWER OF NETWORKING AND SEMINARS
– *"My business really took off in the Internet marketing community when I started going to seminars"*

Stanley: As your website, The Success Doctor, started growing, what were some of the memorable moments you experienced?

Michel: There are memorable moments, I think, for every website. Memorable moments for my practice, for my company The Success Doctor Incorporated, there are quite a few. You mentioned one at the very beginning when you introduced me, which is my letter for John Reese, the Traffic Secrets letter.

Of course, I also wrote the letter for the Underachiever Method for Frank Kern and Ed Dale. It produced around $1 million dollars in about a week. Those were actually the result of going to seminars. For a long time, I wasn't going to any seminars. A lot of the top marketers hired me. I wasn't a marketer, per se; I was a marketing consultant. I was a copywriter and I was hired by all the top marketers.

One day, I went to a seminar just for fun and one of my clients was there and he was one of the speakers. In fact, he was the one who invited me to that seminar. While I was there, he pointed me out in the crowd while he was on stage.

That was a defining moment for me. People, literally, just jumped on me asking me for my business card, asking how I write copy, if I was interested in writing their copy, and that's when my business really took off in the Internet marketing community.

That's when I was able to hang out with top guys like Kirt Christensen, Terry Dean etc. In fact, one of my clients at that time, Stephen Pierce, introduced me to John Reese, who eventually hired me to write the copy that led to my million-dollar-in-one-day sales letter.

TRAFFIC SECRETS:
THE INSIDE STORY OF THE MILLION-DOLLAR-DAY

— *"I'm not necessarily the best copywriter out there, but I feel privileged to have set that record"*

Stanley: A lot of people want to know how you achieved that success. Can you tell us about the story behind John Reese's Traffic Secrets?

Michel: It was probably the longest sales letter I've ever written. The original sales letter was probably around 20 to 25 pages. When we relaunched Traffic Secrets, it was something like 75 pages, because it was filled with testimonials.

It's a sales copy like any other copy. But specifically about that letter was, when I wrote the first draft of the letter, it was actually rejected by John Reese. In fact, I took several months to write that letter and I felt it was good. When I gave it to John Reese, probably a week before the launch of Traffic Secrets, he didn't like it.

He gave me some fantastic reasons why. I learned so much from John. John is a fantastic copywriter himself. He gave me a lot of pointers, he gave me a lot of tips, and he also gave me a lot of copy points that I could expand on and include in the new sales letter.

I said, "OK, I'm going to roll up my sleeves." And literally three days before the big launch, I didn't sleep a single wink. I didn't sleep at all for 72 hours. I literally put myself to work and rewrote the entire Traffic Secrets sales letter just before the launch. Did it pay off? I think history shows that the letter did pay off and made over a million dollars in about, actually, 18 hours.

I'm pretty proud of that because that was a record-setting moment. It broke records at the time, but, of course, that has been beaten many times since then by other very good copywriters like Frank Kern, Harlan Kilstein and Mike Long. They've written sales letters that have made over a million dollars, even several millions of dollars in one day, sometimes in just a few hours.

I guess you can consider my copy for John Reese like the Roger Bannister's four-minute mile record breaker. When Roger Bannister ran the four-minute mile, it was said to be impossible up until that time. That record has been broken again and again since. I guess you could say I feel like I'm the Roger Bannister of online copy. I'm not necessarily the best copywriter out there, but I feel privileged to have set that record.

FROM SERVICE PROVIDER TO INTERNET MARKETER

– *"Rather than trading in hours for dollars, by repurposing the same content that I was using for my services into an actual product, I can now make money with unlimited potential"*

Stanley: Later on, you launched the private membership site called The Copy Doctor. What inspired you to come up with that idea?

Michel: The idea was part fluke and part inspiration. What happened was I was invited to become one of the faculty members of a program by Bob Sterling called The Copy Doctor. It wasn't a membership site. It was a newsletter.

Bob was selling a paid newsletter where he would invite a copywriter from the faculty to do a mini critique on a sales letter of one of the newsletter subscribers. There was Yanik Silver, Alex Mandossian, Paul Lemberg, Brad Peterson and Russ Phelps. There were about 12 top copywriters on that faculty.

What happened was Bob really loved the direct marketing industry, and he wanted to stray away from the copywriting field and dive into the direct marketing field. So he made me an offer and I acquired The Copy Doctor. I wanted to create a private membership site where I didn't have to send out a newsletter, and I would simply post all my critiques there, still in written form. People didn't have to wait for the newsletter to come out and could log in whenever they wanted to and start reading these critiques.

The inspirational part was that there was a seminar that I went to and Armand Morin was actually there, and he introduced me from the stage as being the world's best online copywriter – the best copywriter on the Internet. I felt flattered. What struck me was something he said later. He said, "I go to Michel Fortin's website and I check out his portfolio. It's the best darn swipe file on the Internet."

I thought to myself, "Wow! I should be charging for this." I have people visiting my old sales letters that I had written for John Reese and Stephen Pierce etc. An idea clicked in my head. One of the things I do in my business is I write copy or I critique copy. The way I've critiqued copy nowadays was to do it all on video.

I would literally go through a sales letter for a client and record it on Camtasia – screen-captured video – where I would actually go through the entire sales letter with a microphone and tell this client what's wrong with the sales letter, what's good with the sales letter, and here's what you need to do to your sales letter in order to increase the conversion rate.

These videos were for my clients' eyes only. What I did is slightly change it around. I started to go back to my old clients and say, "Hey, can I have your permission to publish this?" They replied and said, "Sure."

So I put those videos on my membership site, The Copy Doctor. Of course, that eventually transformed into, now, when people hire me, my copywriting service agreement says that I now have the right to publish your materials if I want to. In fact, I charge an extra fee if they want to retain confidentiality.

From that point on, I did critiques on a regular basis. I did two or three of them a month. I would post them to The Copy Doctor membership site. On one hand, a real, paying client actually hires me to critique their copy. And when I'm done, I take that same video and I upload it to The Copy Doctor for my members who pay me on a monthly basis – now they pay me annually – to watch those videos so they can see not only how I write copy, but the logic and the thinking process that I go through when I critique and write copy. A lot of people have told me that it's the best copywriting education they've ever had.

Stanley: So it was a win-win situation for you because you were charging the clients for the critiquing and at the same time you were charging your members for the same critique.

Michel: Exactly, and that was my foray into Internet marketing as an Internet marketer because, up until that point, I was offering services. I was a service provider. I never had a product. I never had sold something that I particularly have created or owned.

I was always offering services. Yes, granted, I charge anywhere between $8,000 to, sometimes, $20,000 for a sales letter. Sometimes, I even have sales letters that have royalties where I get paid a commission for how well the copy performs, but that's still very limited. What I mean by "limited" is because it's basically trading in hours for dollars.

By repurposing the same content that I was using for my services into an actual product, The Copy Doctor, the membership site, I can now make money with unlimited potential where I actually capitalize on my products, on my services, and on the things I've done in exchange for my time.

Now I can capitalize based on the value of that product. That was my very beginning, the foray of becoming an Internet marketer, not just a copywriter. Of course, ever since that time, I've created multiple products and I own several websites and several businesses with my beautiful wife, Sylvie.

FAILURE IS YOUR BIGGEST SUCCESS

— *"When I decided to focus on a tiny niche, that's when I really became successful"*

Stanley: Throughout your copywriting success, what are some failures or mistakes you have made in the past and what lessons did you learn from them?

Michel: I mentioned earlier my first big failure – I think it's not really a failure. To me, it's probably one of my best successes because I'm a positive thinker. It's not just because it's positive thinking; it's because it really was the springboard that led to my success – was my first bankruptcy. I say first because I went bankrupt twice. I was a sales person, I was working on commission, but I was always an employee.

When I decided to go into business for myself when I left my last employer, who was actually a cosmetic surgeon at that time in the early '90s, I created my own company and this was before Success Doctor. I was becoming a freelance marketing consultant. Again, I had to do everything from scratch.

Now I had to go out and find clients rather than find employers. I was doing everything wrong. I was following a lot of the strategies that I taught and everything was fine but, again, it was fear of rejection. There was also the fact that I wasn't really focused on a niche. I was focusing pretty much on anyone who wanted to hire me.

Later on, I realized that I should have focused on a niche, on something that I was passionate about, for example, cosmetic surgery. When I decided to focus only on the cosmetic surgery field and called my company The Success Doctor, because I focused only on doctors, that's when I really became successful.

Before I did that, I was a little naïve. I decided to go after everything. I decided to try to sell my services to everyone, I went bankrupt. My first business went bankrupt because I wasn't successful at all. I wasn't doing well at all. That was my second biggest failure, which eventually led to my second biggest success, which was the creation of my company The Success Doctor and the explosion of my copywriting business, especially online. Those were some of the things that, I guess you could say, I'm even proud of.

But it was tough for eight months prior to my second bankruptcy. I was literally living off of those tiny packages of noodles that you would buy in Chinatown for a quarter, seven days a week for eight months just to survive, because I wasn't making any money at all. I worked on my business so hard. I was working 18 hours a day. Until I realized what I was doing wrong and what things I needed to do in order to do it right, that's when I really took off.

Niche marketing is one big success. This is something that I strongly recommend. I'm not saying that you should focus on niche marketing forever. It's just that it's a great way to start a business. Believe it or not, when you focus on a tiny niche, an industry or a specific type of target market, you get more business. Less is indeed more. The more you focus on fewer clients, the more those clients think or perceive you hold their interest more at heart.

You're more of an expert by default rather than by design because of the fact they think that since you are focused or specialized in a specific area, then you must be an expert. I can say that I'm a marketing consultant, but now if I just say that I'm competing with all the marketing consultants out there, including all the Fortune 500 marketing consultants for big companies like Deloitte & Touche and Anderson Consulting and all those companies.

When I decided to concentrate just on the small, cosmetic surgeons – I became the marketing consultant specializing in cosmetic surgery – my business took off because now almost all the cosmetic surgeons, especially in my area, started to hire me. Of course, I also was hired by cosmetic surgeons in Calgary, Vancouver, Montreal, and then later on I was in the United States.

I went to Florida and stayed there for a while, then New York City, Chicago, L.A., and that's when I realized the power of niche marketing. Now I am pretty much a copy editor online and I don't really focus on any one particular niche. Doing that at the beginning of my career, especially after my second bankruptcy, is what really caused my business to take off. That was one of the things I did right and it's one of the things I highly recommend for people to do as well.

DON'T SET GOALS, SET GUIDES

— *"I believe success is not about reaching a goal; it's really enjoying the process along the way"*

Stanley: Do you set yourself goals?

Michel: I don't believe in setting and achieving goals. I believe in achieving and setting guides. The reason why is that there is a difference between goals and guides. A lot of people set goals. Goals are important because it gives you purpose; it gives you momentum; it gives you an ideal to go after.

But there's a problem with that. What happens if, let's say, you set yourself a goal one year down the road and you could have achieved within six months? You've just limited yourself. In fact, by setting a goal, sometimes it can actually lower your self-esteem, because some people set goals that are so big and lofty that they feel they don't deserve it along the way, so they don't really put their all into it.

Some people abandon their goals. How many New Year's resolutions do people actually keep? Some people do achieve goals when they could have achieved either different goals that were more important, or they could have achieved it in less time. Other people abandon their goals altogether.

So, to me, goals are not important. I want to make sure that people under-stand this. I'm not saying that goal achievement is bad, it's the setting of goals, because people set themselves up for failure if they set only goals. What they should do is find out what's meaningful to them – their inner values and priori-ties in their lives.

If you have priorities, values, passions, or things you love, then you set goals or you set ideals that are backed by those values, so you can use those as guides along the way. Whether you achieve it in six months or one year, it doesn't matter, but along the journey to success, you enjoyed it. You enjoyed the process of reaching your goals.

I believe success is not about reaching a goal; it's really enjoying the pro-cess along the way. A lot of people work so hard and then they discover, once they reach their goals, that they had the wrong goal set in the first place or they changed their mind or say at the end, "Is this it?"

There's an old saying by Lao Tzu, who said that, "Many people climb the ladder of success only to find out at the top that the ladder has been leaning against the wrong wall." That is what I'm trying to say here. You need to find out that you're against the right wall in the first place. What are your values?

If one of the priorities in your life is your family, and you set a career or a business goal, if you keep working on your business goal, guess what's going to happen to your family? You're going to feel either something's wrong or you're going to have a hard time trying to reach your business goals because in the back of your mind, your family is number-one.

It's best to set goals that are in alignment with your family values. And vice versa, if your number-one priority is business, then work on goals that are backed by your business values. My point is don't set goals, set guides.

Guides are basically goals that are in alignment with your priorities, values, passions, things that give you purpose, meaning and fulfillment in your life, in the process of reaching those goals, whether you actually reach those goals or not.

WILL SALES LETTERS AND COPYWRITING STAND THE TEST OF TIME?

– *"Copywriting is about something that is much deeper than copywriting. It's not sales letters, it's not even words - It's selling, it's salesmanship"*

Stanley: Do you think sales letters and copywriting will stand the test of time? Will they be here five years, 10 years, even 20 years from now?

Michel: I can tell you that sales letters have been in existence ever since the beginning of the written word. You and I both know that pretty much the oldest sales letter out there – and there are probably even older ones out there – is the Bible. Of course, copywriting is going to stay around because it's all about something that is much deeper than copywriting.

It's not sales letters, it's not even words. It's selling, it's salesmanship, it's storytelling, the ability to persuade and move audiences, to get them to side with you, to believe in you. In fact, Zig Ziglar says that, "Selling is the transference of enthusiasm that you have for your product into the mind of your prospect."

Well, copywriting is the same thing. It's basically just a written form of doing the exact same thing. You write a sales letter in order to transfer the enthusiasm that the person who is selling the product, into the minds and hearts of the readers, in this particular case. So will copywriting stand the test of time? Absolutely!

It might change in its delivery. Right now we see a lot of video and audio online, and those are basically the same as copywriting, except that now it engages more of the senses. If you have a video online, you still have to write the script, don't you? That's copywriting. It's all copy, but more importantly, it's all about selling.

So will salesmanship stand the test of time? You bet, because it's essential to human survival. I think that if people understand salesmanship, they won't really have to ask that question, because if they learn how to sell, they can learn how to write copy. They can learn to do anything they can in order to start a business, build a business and so on.

So yes, absolutely, it will always stand the test of time – I'm definitely sure of that.

Stanley: Michel, I want to thank you for your time. You've provided us with some excellent content. Do you have any final comments or let people know about your websites where they can get more information about you?

Michel: Thank you, Stanley. I appreciate you giving me the time. If people want to know more about what I do an offer, there are two websites. One is for my copywriting services and that's SuccessDoctor.com. The other one is my membership site for if they're interested in learning about copywriting at TheCopyDoctor.com.

CHAPTER 7

YANIK SILVER:
Autopilot Web Business Expert

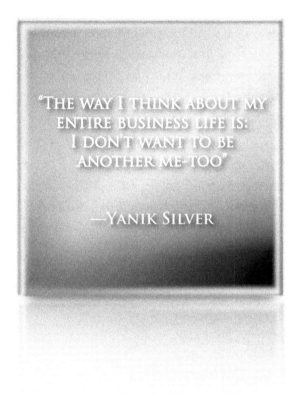

"THE WAY I THINK ABOUT MY
ENTIRE BUSINESS LIFE IS:
I DON'T WANT TO BE
ANOTHER ME-TOO"

—YANIK SILVER

AT THREE O'CLOCK IN THE MORNING, YANIK SILVER WOKE UP *with a crazy idea to create this simple two-page website. When he told his friends about it, they were rolling on the floor laughing – and they had every right to be amused since he had absolutely no web design skills, zero HTML or coding knowledge.*

121

But that didn't stop the self-proclaimed computer dunce from going ahead. Starting from his one-bedroom apartment and with only $1,800 invested, he registered the domain name InstantSalesLetters.com and launched it one month later.

It was an instant success and he earned back his $1,800 investment within the very first month. The next month, he made $3,600 and then $7,300 the next month. By the fourth month, he has already made over $9,400 and was well on track to do six figures that year. At that point, everyone wanted to know how he did it.

Seeing a bigger opportunity just waiting to be capitalized, Yanik began to create his own information products helping other aspiring entrepreneurs achieve the high levels of success he was experiencing. Now, he has now sold everything from e-books on fitness, drawing techniques and houseplants to $20,000+ Mastermind programs, built an affiliate program of 44,000 members, and generated more traffic to his homemade, barebones sites than huge multi-national conglomerates.

Today, Yanik is recognized as the leading expert on creating automatic, money making websites and has personally sold over $12,000,000 online and counting (with zero employees except his wife, Missy). He has been featured on the cover of Millionaire Blueprints magazine, inside Business 2.0, TIME. com, About.com, Staples.com, Internet.com, SmartMoney.com, Denver Business Journal and others.

To Yanik, he has achieved the ultimate Internet lifestyle of fun, freedom and financial independence.

THE 14 YEAR-OLD ENTREPRENEUR

— *"That was my incubator, my place to experiment and learn these direct response techniques"*

Stanley: Tell us a bit about your childhood and where you came from.

Yanik: Actually my family is from Russia. We're Russian immigrants and we came over when I was two-and-a-half years old. My dad is kind of like the typical immigrant success story that has become famous now. He came over with only $256 in his pocket for my mom, her mom and me.

He went to work at a job here repairing medical equipment. On the side, he started repairing medical equipment for doctors that worked at the hospital. The hospital administrators found out about this and told him he had to quit doing that or else he was going to get fired. He decided to go off on his own and started his own medical equipment repair business. It turned into Medical Equipment Sales and Service.

Growing up, I was always involved in that business. Growing up in a family business, you pretty much do anything that you've got to do there. When I was about 14 years old, I started telemarketing for him to sell latex gloves. I handled cold calling on the doctors myself via telephone; I'd follow up on my own leads; I'd send out samples; I'd close my own sales and get commissions. So I really started getting into sales early on. I didn't like it but I did it because I had to.

When I was 16, I got my driver's license and went out and made cold calls on doctors in person. I still can't believe that they talked to a little 16 year-old punk. But I knew a whole lot about medical equipments and talked to them about it. I decided there's got to be a better way and one of my doctor clients actually gave me a Jay Abraham tape. It was all about direct response marketing. I thought, "Wow, this is pretty incredible. I can send out a letter or a fax – now an email – and have people take some sort of action."

I was just enthralled by that. I started studying as much as I possibly could to get really good at these techniques of direct marketing. I'd write these full page ads for my dad's business and he'd look at me and say, "Nobody is going to read all this," in his Russian accent. I'd say, "Come on Dad, let's just try it."

We'd run these full page ads and fax them to our customers. We'd have people sending back credit cards for buying equipments that before we could only sell via in person. We were selling from an ad and getting them to raise their hand and say, "Yeah, I want to take a look at this." It really changed the entire aspect of his business.

Stanley: What did you learn from the experience back then, helping with your dad's business?

Yanik: That was my incubator, my place to experiment and learn these direct response techniques. I started getting an itch to go off on my own and began consulting with my doctor clients that I was working with to help them get more patients. I used the same techniques there and it was working really well so I thought, "Well, I can keep doing this and essentially get paid by the hour as a consultant, or I can package it off and sell it to other doctors all across the country."

That's pretty much when I started learning from Dan Kennedy, Jeff Paul and some other people about information marketing. I thought, "This is kind of cool." So I decided to sell a course to cosmetic surgeons and dermatologists on how to get more patients. I was going to charge $900 for this three-ring binder of information.

To me, at that point, I thought it was kind of crazy but I thought I'd go for it. We got 10 leads out of this one little classified ad I ran and one doctor ordered on the last day of the deadline. I was so excited. I couldn't believe it. So I had to go to work creating the product. I told the doctor that I'm not going to charge his card and within 30 days I'd be republishing it.

GOING ONLINE: A CRAZY IDEA AT
THREE O'CLOCK IN THE MORNING THAT MADE SIX FIGURES

– *"It sounds like an overnight success story but actually it started way back when I was 14 years old"*

So that was the very first sale I made in the information marketing business. That business quickly grew to about $10,000 to $15,000 a month – I was probably 25 or 26 years old at the time – and that's when I left my dad's business and started really paying attention to the Internet.

I thought, "This is kind of cool. I see people out there selling information on the Internet and there's no shipping cost, no delivery cost – a lot of stuff is digitally delivered. I can do that. Why don't I have the sales letter up on there?"

I'm a big believer in questions. So I asked myself the question, "How can I create a fully automatic web business that makes me money while I sleep and is an incredible value to others?" It can't just be an e-book. I wanted something to differentiate myself.

And, literally, at three o'clock in the morning, I got the answer. I poked my wife with my finger and said, "Miss, Miss, wake up! I got this great idea!" She said, "Oh, God, please go back to bed." I said, "No, this is going to be good!" I jumped out of bed and registered a domain name, which was InstantSalesLetters.com, and went to work on it right away.

That was my very first online business which took me about a month to get started. Like you mentioned in the introduction, I started with only $1,800 from my one bedroom apartment, which sounds like an infomercial. I woke up one morning and had $60 sitting in my email account – it was a $29.95 product at that time – and I was like, "Wow, this is amazing!"

I made about $1,800 in my first month, then about $3,600 in the next month, then about $7,300 in the next month, and then about $9,400 the fourth month. I was on track to do over six figures and that's when people were asking, "How the hell did you do that? What did you do?"

It sounds like an overnight success story, but actually it started way back when I was 14 years old.

Stanley: When was this back in?

Yanik: This was 2000 and I thought I was kind of late to the party. Even today, a lot of people think that they're extremely late to the party on the Internet and don't believe that they might be able to do what I've done.

I think, truthfully, that right now is an even better time to start online, because there are more roadmaps to follow if you find the right people who have integrity and walk their talk. There are easier tools; there are quicker ways of getting out there; there are more buyers who are comfortable buying online. I think it's a great time.

I actually just came out with a book called *Moonlighting on the Internet*. That's a real bookstore book. It's probably the best $15 you'll ever spend on how to get up and going with making money online.

A COMPUTER DUNCE

– *"You learn as you go and you learn more from action than sitting around thinking about it"*

Stanley: What were some initial obstacles you faced down? How did you overcome them?

Yanik: The biggest obstacle was that I didn't know what the hell I was doing. You learn as you go and you learn more from action than sitting around thinking about it. I had a handful of resources that I found that made sense to me and I used those as guidelines.

I went around looking at what people were doing that seemed successful. Marlon Sanders and Kenny Boyd were some of the first people that I really looked at. Today, Marlon and I are now good friends, which is kind of interesting to see that come around full circle. It's kind of cool that the people who I looked up to, I've become pretty good friends with now.

My biggest obstacle is, I call myself a computer dunce. It's the truth. I don't know how to put up my own website, yet my life is depended on it. But I found people who could do that for me. I concentrated on the things that I was good at, which was writing copy, product creation, and, later on, creating relationships and partnerships.

THE POWER OF VIRAL MARKETING
— *"I think your customers determine what goes viral"*

Stanley: After the Instant Sales Letter, what did you do next?

Yanik: I like experiments, so I wanted to create an e-book that would get virally passed along. I came up with this idea called *Autoresponder Magic*. If you do a search for "Autoresponder Magic" on Google, I don't know how many tens of thousands of references to that thing now.

What I did is it's really a compilation product. I thought people were having issues creating autoresponder sequences, so I would go to people who had successful autoresponder sequences and asked them if I could put them in an e-book. They would get publicity because their things are out there being exposed to people. I just compiled it along with some instruction on how to use autoresponders.

I no longer to this, but at that time, I sold it for $17 and I let people have the rights to it so they could sell it too. As soon as they bought it, they could go around and resell it, or give it away, or do whatever they wanted.

This was what made that thing explode and got my name out there everywhere, which wasn't my original intention, but it worked well for that. My original intention was really – I was an affiliate for each of the people that were in the e-book – to make affiliate commissions from that. That worked out OK.

The next generation was this book called *Million Dollar Emails*, which was the same thing with the best producing emails. That worked out a little bit better. I got a little bit smarter about the way I clipped affiliate links in there, and even smarter the next time I did a resell rights product.

Stanley: Speaking of viral e-books, what do you think is the biggest key to the success of a viral marketing campaign?

Yanik: It's changed a lot recently and I don't really think that I'm a real huge viral expert by any stretch. I think your customers determine what goes viral. I've really tried to work the viral angle from combining it with my affiliate program, which I'm really strong at. We have about 44,000 some affiliates. I try and create content that people can get paid on for distributing.

Also, if I create a viral e-book, I want people who are distributing it to be able to quickly create an affiliate link inside there and create a PDF. I had some custom programming developed that is at www.viralebookcreator.com, which is kind of cool. We don't sell that; we just use it ourselves. People can enter their affiliate ID number in and out will pop a PDF e-book that they can use to virally pass along and give to their subscribers or website visitors or anything like that.

I've always done it as far as a monetary incentive. That's not going to get you the huge viral pass along that you've seen just recently with the OfficeMax campaign with the dancing elves. You've probably seen that one, Stanley, during the holidays?

Stanley: Yeah.

Yanik: Everyone puts their picture on the little dancing elf and the elf will dance around and do these dumb dances. Stuff like that is going to be viral because people want to keep passing it along to their friends because it's funny. I've never really focused that much on anything like that. I focus more on creating tools for my affiliates to pass along.

UNDERGROUND ONLINE SEMINAR

— *"Something else that I really try and do with my business is make it fun for our customers and subscribers, and don't be boring because that's the worst thing you could possibly do in marketing"*

Stanley: After the viral e-book, what was your next product or project?

Yanik: I got invited to speak at a seminar and I didn't have anything to sell there. I decided that a lot of people would probably want to know how I did what I did. I presold a tell-all type program teaching people how to take their expertise or any information that they wanted and sell it online. I did, pretty much, the same thing I did with the doctor's manual: Sold it first then decided to go make it.

I told people at the seminar that this was a prepublication type offer. I didn't sell too many; I made something like $8,000. So it wasn't very exciting, but it was exciting enough at the time to make me create this manual. It was called *Instant Internet Profits*. It's no longer available. But that was my first kind of tell-all, "let me teach you want I've been doing" type course.

After that, there have been a lot of spin-offs of projects, like 33 Days to Online Profits. Then I created a little fitness e-book, as a joint venture with my personal trainer, just as a great example of content that you can create even if you're not the expert in something. It's called *Get Fit While You Sit*. I can't even remember how the rest of the products all shook out.

Stanley: Speaking of seminars, you founded the seminar called Underground Online Seminar. Can you tell us what inspired you to start that?

Yanik: Absolutely. I mean, there's no shortage of Internet marketing seminars out there. When I finally decided that I was going to run my own seminar, I thought, "I really want to do something different."

The way I think about my entire business life is: I don't want to be another me-too. I don't want to create another product that's just like somebody else's out there. There's no differentiation point. There's pretty much no reason for existence, unless you want to play the game of low price, and I don't like playing that game.

Every market is competitive now, so you've got to have a big idea. The big idea for the Underground Online Seminar is going the opposite direction. So, while other Internet seminars pretty much have the same lineup of speakers, gurus and experts that you see all the time, the Underground Online Seminar are these real-world people, who are making millions of dollars online, but, for the most part, nobody has ever heard of them. They're just kind of quietly working in the shadows, doing their own thing.

And because I'm friends with a lot of different guys and gals – now friends of friends of friends – it's grown every single year. We've been able to get more and more, higher and higher caliber talent to come out. It's really become this pretty exciting event. It's just a once a year thing that I do.

We also have a lot of fun with it. That's something else that I really try and do with my business is make it fun for our customers and subscribers. And don't be boring, because that's the worst thing you could possibly do in marketing. People are excited to hear from you, if you've got something exciting to tell them.

So I'll run sales. For instance, when my son was born, it was the "Baby Z" sale. His name was Zak. We'd run a sale for that. My daughter Zoe was born eight months ago, so we ran another "Baby Z" sale for her. I've done things like "Save Yanik's Marriage" sale. So, keeping things interesting fit into my personality.

The Underground Online Seminar is no exception. We have a ton of fun there. It's a whole spy theme and I really play the spy theme over the top. Each year, it becomes a different spy theme. This year, the theme is 24 and we're bringing in the actor, Carlos Bernard, who plays Tony Almeida. The year before, we brought in Peter Graves from Mission Impossible. The year before that, we brought in Verne Troyer, who plays Mini-Me on Austin Powers. Keeping it fun and exciting for people is a big deal.

HOW TO COME UP WITH IDEAS
FOR YOUR INFORMATION PRODUCTS

– *"You don't need to be a world-class expert to sell information on a particular subject. You've just got to be a little bit more knowledgeable than the average person"*

Stanley: You're a huge expert in creating information products. Do you have a formula or a strategy to come up with the flood of ideas for your information products?

Yanik: I don't know if I have a formula, per se. I have some guidelines. There are two ways of looking at where to come up with ideas:

1. **Your own life.** In your own life you want to think about: What am I good at? What do I really like to do? What are my passions about? What do people ask me about? What have been my previous jobs? Going down, almost like a resume-like thing: What have I done? What do I know about more than the average person?

   That's a key point: You don't need to be a world-class expert to sell information on a particular subject; you've just got to be a little bit more knowledgeable, for the most part, than the average person.

   I also think about: What are my pains? Where are pain points? *The Get Fit While You Sit* product came from a story that I saw on CNN about how traffic had grown exponentially in the U.S. I thought, "It'd be cool to create a fitness product that people could do while they're in their cars, hanging out in traffic."

   My trainer was like, "Yeah, that's a bad idea. We'll get sued by the first person that gets rear-ended by this guy doing exercises in his car." So that transformed into exercises you could do while watching TV or sitting at the computer. Something like that is where I come up with ideas.

2. **From the outside.** The other way is from the outside and thinking about: Who are my friends that have interesting skill sets? Who could I get a hold of that has interesting skill sets?

   And then finding marketplaces, where people are already spending money, where they're already passionate, and where they're reachable – so, golfers, investors, people looking to make extra money, all those. Pretty much anything that has sold for the last 100 years via mail order is a good marketplace to consider.

MAVERICK BUSINESS ADVENTURES

— *"I really wanted to create a club of more people like me, who are successful entrepreneurs and CEOs, who are into adventure"*

Stanley: You've got something interesting coming up called Maverick Business Adventures. Can you tell us a little about that and what inspired you to start that?

Yanik: Thanks for asking about that. That's my absolute favorite thing right now, where I'm spending the majority of my energy and time on. I've always been into adventures and once-in-a-lifetime experiences and all sorts of adrenaline type things: Bungee jumping, running with the bulls, skydiving, you name it. I even signed up for the Virgin Galactic space flight!

I really wanted to create a club of more people like me – successful entrepreneurs and CEOs who are into adventure. I couldn't find that so I created it myself of a group of people who are interested in that and, at the same time, combining it with business networking, business building, entrepreneurial type workshops and also a third part, which is really important to me, is giving back.

So it's once-in-a-lifetime experiences combined with the business building stuff. Also, each trip we do a session for young entrepreneurs in the area, teaching them from the members who volunteer with their real world advice. That's going to expand. We also do a charity aspect for entrepreneurial charities where 5 percent of revenue from that business goes to them.

It's something that I'm extremely passionate about because it encompasses pretty much my whole life, for the most part, of everything that I'm really into from entrepreneurship in business to adventure.

We also bring a celebrity icon on every trip. Last time, we brought Jesse James. We also offered an experience with about 800 miles Baja racing in Mexico and Jesse James was there for two of those days. We taught kids from a local college in Cabo. It's a lot of fun and very rewarding as well.

CRACKING THE SEVEN-FIGURE MARK

— *"[Don't] wait for somebody to anoint you an expert or a leader. It's your job to go out there and proclaim yourself such, as long as you got the knowledge and the wear-with-all to back it up"*

Stanley: A lot of people have no problem making five or six-figures every year online, but 99 percent of them just don't seem to be able to crack that seven-figure mark. What do you think is the difference between a six-figure business, and a seven or eight-figure business?

Yanik: Well I can't comment on the eight figure business, except for my friends that are doing it. I've kept my business for the most part small in the multiple of seven-figures, just so I can keep it more of a lifestyle business. But probably the biggest thing is not techniques or strategy or anything like that; it's more about what's going on in your head.

There's a book called *Winning by Intimidation* by Robert Ringer, which he's recently re-released and gave it a worse title called *To Be or Not to Be Intimated*. I don't know if this section is in there, I'd assume it is, but there's something in there called The Leapfrog Theory.

The Leapfrog Theory says that you're not to wait for somebody to anoint you an expert or a leader or anything like that. It's your job to go out there and proclaim yourself such, as long as you got the knowledge and the wear-with-all to back it up, or else you're going to be back in the heap with the mediocre majority pretty soon.

Many people are waiting for somebody to give them permission. You don't need permission. It's inside your head. You've got to essentially decide, "That's what I'm going to do." Then just go ahead and step up to that position of leadership, of being a seven-figure business — What does that mean? What are the things that have to happen to do that?

The obvious thing is going back to the questions. You can keep asking yourself the questions, "How am I going to reach that seven-figure level?" For me, that became selling, for the most part, a smaller amount of people but higher dollar amounts. So higher priced seminars, higher priced programs. We have even as high as a $20,000 mastermind program that we sell. So raising the prices was one way that I've done it.

Stanley: Yanik, I want to thank you for your time. Do you have any final comments you want to add, or let people know about your main website, where to get more information about you?

Yanik: They can just go to InternetLifestyle.com and read my blog there. That's about it. The biggest thing I can tell people is just go out there and do it. If you're succeeding already in a small way, just go out there and succeed in a big way. If you haven't got started yet, just go out there and realize that there's never going to be a perfect time regardless of what you might think.

A lot of people wait until they believe there is going to be some perfect time to start their online business, or whatever venture they want to do. The truth is, Stanley, as you know, there is never a perfect time. You just got to get out there and do it and make it happen.

CHAPTER 8

STU MCLAREN:
Affiliate Management Expert

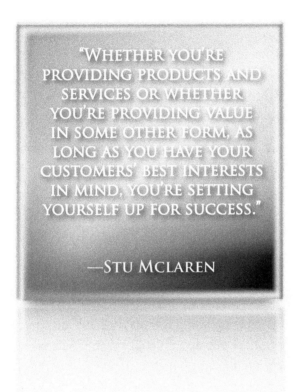

"WHETHER YOU'RE PROVIDING PRODUCTS AND SERVICES OR WHETHER YOU'RE PROVIDING VALUE IN SOME OTHER FORM, AS LONG AS YOU HAVE YOUR CUSTOMERS' BEST INTERESTS IN MIND, YOU'RE SETTING YOURSELF UP FOR SUCCESS."

—STU MCLAREN

ARMED WITH NOTHING MORE THAN A FUNDAMENTAL KNOWL-*edge of online marketing and basic HTML... Stu Mclaren became one of the most sought-after and highest paid affiliate managers on the web in just nine short months.*

And ever since, he has been behind the scenes managing and consulting on some of the biggest affiliate campaigns and product launches around. In fact, just recently, he helped one of his clients generate over $1 million-dollars in less than 29 days.

Today, he consults, trains and educates small business owners on how to build a profitable affiliate program that generates leads and sales and increases bottom-line profits.

How did he achieve all this? Here's the behind-the-scenes story of Stu Mclaren, how his creative thinking system works, and how you can put it to work for you.

A CREATIVE THINKER IS BORN

— *"Creative thinking was, for me, a turning point"*

Stanley: Stu, let's start off with your college life and tell us how it eventually led you to Internet marketing.

Stu: Sure. I went to university to study business administration. We had a pretty good business program, but for everybody out there who's ever been in a program where things are quite competitive, I'm sure you can relate to this. My first year, I didn't really do as well as I probably should have. I was playing soccer for the university team and my focus was not on school work; it was more on soccer itself, so my grades suffered.

Even though I passed all of my classes, I didn't have the average to continue on in the program. I got that little slip that comes back and says, "You may no longer proceed in this program." That was a setback for me and it upset me up a little bit. I managed to talk my way back into the program – I spoke to a couple of professors and I did a couple of extra assignments and bumped my marks up – and I was able to get back in.

The second year wasn't much better, but the third year everything changed for me. My marks went sky high. I had a lot more success in my class. By the end of my fourth year, I graduated with honors and was named "Most Outstanding Male" of my graduating class.

The major difference for me at that point in time was learning about how to develop my creative abilities. In one of our classes, we saw a video from a gentleman by the name of Doug Hall. He owns and runs a company called Eureka Ranch, where Fortune 500 companies come to his facility and they brainstorm for three days and come up with new product ideas.

What was so amazing to me was the fact that, here's a guy who is running around in shorts and a T-shirt, shooting Nerf guns at corporate CEOs and they're playing all these fun games, and he's getting paid $150,000 for three days of brainstorming. To me, that really looked intriguing, so I decided to explore it a little more and started to learn a lot more about creative thinking. That really, for me, was a turning point because it helped turn around my schoolwork and it's paid dividends many times over in my business.

Shortly after graduating, I was lined up to head into the corporate world. I had actually signed a contract with a big company up here in Canada. Everything on paper looked great. I had great pay, a company car, benefits – you name it, I had it. But something just wasn't sitting right for me. I don't know whether it's your instinct or your gut or what, but something was telling me that it wasn't the right path.

I decided to spend some time exploring those thoughts. I made the decision to resign before I even started. I didn't know what I was going to do, I didn't know how I was going to do it, but I decided to go out and speak professionally to colleges and high-school students about how to use creativity in their schoolwork and their lives to get whatever job they wanted.

That really was the major turning point for me, making that decision. From there, that's led to speaking all around the world on creativity. I knew the value of learning from others. I found some mentors who guided me in a direction that has blossomed into the business that I now have today.

THE POWER OF CREATIVE THINKING

— *"One of the main principles of creative thinking is not so much coming up with fancy-dancy creative techniques; it's utilizing questions that get your mind going in a direction that it otherwise would not have"*

Stanley: Can you talk a bit about what is creative thinking?

Stu: I think the real gem, when it comes to creative thinking, is the fact that when you start applying creative thinking techniques and just spending the time to think and brainstorm about certain challenges you may have in your life, the reality is you can literally, any time you want to, come up with some type of a solution or idea to get what it is that you want.

Here's a quick example: When I was starting out my speaking career, I mentioned that one of the things that I knew early on was that I needed to learn from people who were at a level that I wanted to get to. One of those individuals was a speaker in a local speaking organization here in Canada called CAPS, which is the Canadian Association for Professional Speakers.

I said to him, "Chris, I want to get to your level. I want to be a speaker who is out there speaking to the world. What do I need to do now to get to where you are as quick as possible?" He said, "One of the first things you should do is join this organization. The second thing you should do is you need to get out to our national conference."

At that particular time, we had this conversation around October and the national conference was early December. The problem that I had was it was on the complete opposite side of Canada. I had just graduated from university. I didn't have any money, shoulder deep in student debt, and I'm just starting this business so there was very little income coming in.

The idea of being able to not only pay for my flight, hotel, and meals and get out there was one thing, but then to pay for the registration at the event was an entirely new concept that for me just wasn't feasible at that time. What I did was I went back and joined the organization. Then I asked myself a key question.

I said, "How can I get out to this particular conference?" One of the main principles of creative thinking is not so much coming up with fancy-dancy creative techniques, but instead is about utilizing questions that get your mind going in a direction that it otherwise would not have. This particular question, "How can I get out to that conference?" really got me thinking.

One of the things that I realized was, "What do I have right now that other people don't have and would want?" At that particular time, I had time available. I was just out of university, I was just starting my business, so I had more time than money. One of the things I did was brainstorm on it and developed a whole campaign which I called: Help Stu, Help You.

Essentially what I did was I got up in front of this local organization and I asked for five minutes of time. I first started off asking them, "How many of you started off your speaking career with very little experience?" Obviously, all their hands are going to be up. Then I said, "Of those who have your hands up, how many of you have been out to the CAPS national conference before?"

About three-quarters of the room kept their hands in the air. I said, "Of those, how many of you would feel it would be valuable for someone like myself, just starting out, to be at that particular conference?" Well, they all kept their hands in the air.

I said, "Great, here's a proposal for you. I know that as professional speakers, one of the things you don't have is time. Unfortunately, that's one of the things I have an abundance of at this particular point. What I'm willing to do is trade my time for a financial contribution of your choice. I'll make phone calls for you. I'll write letters for you. I'll follow up on sales leads for you. I'll mow your grass. Heck, I'll even wipe your baby's bottom, if that need be, for a financial contribution of your choice."

What happened was immediately after I said that, a gentleman from the back of the room stood up and he said, "I'll pay for your flight to get out to the conference." I was floored. Somebody just stood up right at that point and offered to pay for my entire flight to get all the way across Canada.

Immediately afterwards, another gentleman popped up and said, "I'll pay for the cost to attend the seminar itself." Boom, boom, right away, I pretty much had three quarters of my entire cost covered by two gentlemen all because of a little campaign that I did. One of the key components of that was immediately afterwards, a gentleman who offered to pay for my flight – the first gentleman who stood up – gave me a copy of his book.

In the book, there was a section that said, "You have the right to ask," and he circled it. He said, "Stu, I'm rewarding you, because there are many people who have wanted to go to that conference, but have just never had the courage to get up there, do something about it, and ask for what it is that they wanted. I want to reward you for that, because that's part of the learning and growing process."

It just goes to demonstrate that had I not sat down and brainstormed on how I could get out to this conference versus consuming myself with negative thoughts of, "Oh, I wish I could go but I can't because I don't have any money," and blah, blah, blah. There are so many excuses that life can give you, but the decision to find a solution to any challenges that you have comes from within and comes from asking yourself key questions and then brainstorming on ideas to get beyond those particular challenges.

It really boils down to asking yourself key questions and then surrounding yourself with what is called stimuli. Stimuli can be anything that you can see, touch, taste, or hear – things that get your mind moving in a direction. The reason stimuli are so important to the creative process is because they start to naturally feed your brain with ideas.

If you're thinking of a new product idea for your particular company, for example, if you started looking at similar products, products of your competitors, or if you looked at questions that were coming into your support desk or things of that nature, what's going to happen is you're going to start to see and think of all different kinds of ideas.

In that creative process, the important component is capturing all of those ideas whether it is writing them down, recording them, or what have you. You want to record all of your ideas because in and amongst all of those ideas will be a few gems and those are the ones that you really want to pursue.

Creative thinking is nothing more than taking the time to think and brainstorm, asking yourself key questions, surrounding yourself with lots of stimuli, both related to your problem or challenge and stimuli that are not related at all to your problem or challenge, because that will help you come up with unique ideas. Finally, you need to capture all of those ideas and concepts and pursue the few gems that come from it as a result.

BECOMING AN AFFILIATE MANAGER

— *"As an affiliate manager, our role is basically to help serve the needs of our affiliates and to help them sell more of our products, more often, and more frequently"*

Stanley: After you started your speaking career, how did you get introduced to the Internet?

Stu: One of the things I mentioned earlier was that I knew that it was important for me to surround myself with mentors who were doing what it was that I wanted to do. In starting my speaking business, I realized that there was a maximum amount that I would be able to earn as a speaker.

High schools and colleges could only afford to pay so much each time I spoke at their schools and I could only do so many speaking engagements in a year. Multiply those two together and that was the maximum amount that I was able to earn each and every year. I didn't want to settle for that. I wanted to go beyond that so I started to look for alternative ways to generate revenue as a speaker.

That led me to a person by the name of John Childers. John is world renowned for teaching people how to build a multi-million dollar speaking business, so I started to learn from him. To make another very long story short, I found a creative way to get to his particular training. That was an important point in time for me because I learned a tremendous amount at that training.

It literally tripled the amount that I was earning per speaking engagement almost instantly, which was great. Then I went back to his training again as a volunteer because, at that time if you went to the training you could come back again. I went again and, this time, I had a different objective because John has so many people come through his trainings, he didn't know me from Adam or Bob.

So my goal was to be able to get John Childers to know who Stu McLaren was. At that training, I asked for five minutes of his time, and during those five minutes, I shared with him different ideas on how I felt he could grow his business. I had done some brainstorming and creative thinking ahead of time and showed him those ideas.

During that meeting, he didn't really seem too excited about the ideas. I felt almost let down. I thought this was my big moment, this was going to be it. But he only said, "Thanks" and that was it. Then shortly afterwards, a member of his staff came up to me and said, "Stu, are you available to meet with John for breakfast tomorrow morning?"

I remembered looking down at my calendar and then I looked right up and said, "Let me check my calendar. Oh, yes, of course! I'm available." We met and we chatted and we talked. We discussed the concepts of what I was doing with the creative thinking and he was very intrigued by that. That conversation led to me working with John shortly after that.

He asked if I would join his team and I did. I was working virtually from Canada. I guess I was doing a few things right, because a few months later he actually asked me to move down to Fulton, Mississippi, where his office is based, to work with him full time and take on a much bigger role. By doing that, I was then working with him full time in Fulton, Mississippi.

We lived down there for a-year-and-a-half, because both my now wife and my sister and brother-in-law came down and worked with us. It was a very good experience, because John was running a multi-million dollar company and many of the people who speak at his seminars were Internet marketers.

I became very close with two of those individuals. One was Alex Mandossian and the second was Armand Morin. Those two guys really introduced me to the concept of marketing products and services on the Internet. That led to me exploring that further with my speaking business.

Afterwards, when I decided to spread my wings, if you will, and go out on my own, Alex scooped me up right away and asked me if I would be interested in doing affiliate management for him. At the time, I had no idea what affiliate management was, but he said I had the perfect characteristics for it.

He said, "You're good with people. You have a fairly decent technical knowledge that you're not going to get hung up. You're very creative and you're a great trainer. All of those are vital components of affiliate management and I would love to hire you for it." He did and we did a few things right.

We helped him generate over a million bucks in 29 days with his affiliates and, from that point forward, word spread and, ever since, we were in the affiliate management business. We've been very successful. We've been very fortunate to work with some top-tier clients. You mentioned some of them – Mark Victor Hansen, Armand Morin, Alex Mandossian, and so forth.

Through that, we've learned a tremendous amount. It's not only helped my particular business but it's helped all of my clients as well. It's been a great ride and we've really enjoyed it. That was how I was introduced to Internet marketing.

Stanley: You mentioned affiliate management. A lot of listeners might not know what affiliate management is. Can you give us a quick explanation?

Stu: The easiest way to think about it is to think of a traditional business that has a sales force. All of those sales people need to be coordinated and managed by somebody. Typically, it's a sales manager. That sales manager creates materials for them, trains them on how to best sell those products and services, and is there to motivate and guide them in selling those products and services on a regular basis.

Similarly, an affiliate manager is almost identical to a sales manager. The only difference is the sales people are virtual. The virtual sales people are the affiliates and the affiliate manager is just like the sales manager. We're there to help guide our affiliates, train them, and provide materials and resources to help them best sell our products and services.

The key component of it is that we're there to do the thinking for them. The easier you can make it for your affiliates to sell your products and services, the more likely they're going to sell them for you. As an affiliate manager, our role is basically to help serve the needs of our affiliates and to help them sell more of our products, more often, and more frequently.

Many people have an affiliate program online, but typically they're managing it themselves, if they're managing it at all. Most affiliate programs are grossly neglected online and it's a shame, because a lot of product owners are leaving so much money on the table. When you have a well managed affiliate program, the results that you can get are exponential when you compare it to one that is being neglected.

Most product owners set up an affiliate program, maybe create one set of tools, and then after that point, they just leave it and hope that the affiliates are going to continuously promote their products and services. The truth of the matter is, if you're looking to really grow your business, you don't want to sit there and hope your affiliates are going to promote your products and services. You want to be able to ensure that they're going to promote it month in and month out. The only way you do that is by managing your affiliate program.

An affiliate manager is very similar to a sales manager in the traditional sense. We're there to motivate our affiliates, train them, and provide tools and resources that our affiliates can use in their promotions.

HOW TO MOTIVATE AFFILIATES

— *"The more you can look out for your affiliates, the more they're likely to promote"*

Stanley: What are some ways to motivate affiliates?

Stu: There are many ways to motivate affiliates. The key is really finding out what motivates them. Different people are going to be motivated by different ways:

1. **Easy to promote.** Some affiliates are motivated by the fact that, your program may be easier to promote, so there's less work involved. So the more work you can do up front for the affiliates, the more likely they're going to promote.

2. **Money.** Others are purely motivated by money. If your affiliate program pays out higher commission, that's going to get their interest so they're more likely to promote you if they can earn more.

3. **Contests.** Likewise, other affiliates are really motivated by contests. You'll see this all the time particularly during product launches. I want to encourage everybody to do it on a regular basis and that's by having regular contests and prizes. Perhaps you could have a promotion where certain affiliates are given certain prizes if they meet certain criteria. Or the top five or top 10 affiliates during a particular promotion get a prize.

   I've even seen great contests where the affiliate manager or product owner rewarded all affiliates no matter what level they were, whether they generated a whole bunch of sales or just a few, based on their improvement over their average monthly sales. If there was an affiliate who wasn't generating any sales each month and all of the sudden they generated five, they would get a prize the same as the affiliate who perhaps is generating 20 sales a month and who now generated 45.

   The key is finding contests and creating promotions and creating reasons for your affiliates to mail out and coupling that with a good reason and motivation to promote you with prizes and things of that nature.

4. **Surprise bonuses and prizes.** The other thing that I've seen that increases affiliate loyalty is when you give surprise bonuses and priz-

es. Just sending your affiliates gift certificates to Amazon.com or to a steakhouse or things of that nature really not only surprises the affiliate, but it also increases their loyalty because they know you're looking out for their best interests. At the end of the day that's what it really boils down to. The more you can look out for your affiliates, the more they're likely to promote.

5. **Constant communication.** The other key thing is when you're looking to motivate your affiliates is that you want to stay in constant communication with them. If you don't communicate with your affiliates on a regular basis, they're going to move on to some other program.

    If you stay in front of your affiliates, communicate with them, find out what they need and then you help provide those things they need to promote your products and services, there's a much higher probability that they're going to do it.

    You want to stay in communication. You want to talk to your affiliates and find out, "What do you need? What can we do to help you to sell our products more effectively and more often?" When you do that, you're going to find out all the little things that will motivate each individual affiliate.

    I'm not saying you need to communicate with every single one, but I am saying that you want to make a practice of communicating regularly to all of your affiliates, perhaps doing surveys or ASK campaigns, where they can submit their questions, and find out what is really going on in their minds and then look to help them as much as possible.

THE FOUR MAIN INGREDIENTS TO SUCCESS

— *"Amateurs focus on the first sale" (Mike Litman)*

Stanley: What do you think are the key main ingredients to success as an Internet marketer?

Stu: I believe there are four main keys to success as an Internet marketer:

1. **Understanding the lifetime value of your customers and prospects.** A lot of people miss the boat on this. If you develop a strong relationship with your customers, you're then going to be in a position to be able to take that one-time sale into multiple purchases. You hear it time and time again that it's much easier to sell a product to somebody who already knows, likes, and trusts you and those are you customers, especially if you do your job right.

   If you're there just to screw your customer, then obviously that relationship's not going to be where it needs to be. You want to always have the customer's best interest in mind. When you approach business with the mindset that you're there to help your customers, serve your customers, and provide value to your customers on a regular basis, then you're in a good position to build those lifelong relationships.

   When you understand the lifetime value of a customer, you approach business completely differently. You're no longer focused on the first sale. In fact, Mike Litman is famous for saying, "Amateurs focus on the first sale." Professionals realize that the first sale is just the beginning. In fact, if we break even on the first sale, we're happy with that because that gives us an opportunity to demonstrate the value that we can provide that particular customer.

   As such, the next time around when we offer products and services, the conversion rates are going to be much higher, because that customer knows the types of value that we can provide. So understanding the lifetime value of customers is critically important.

2. **Understanding the value of continuous list building and relationship building.** This works for both online and offline businesses. In fact, I have a good friend of mine who runs an offline restaurant.

One of the things he came to me and said was, "Stu, listen, I know you're involved in marketing. I was wondering if you could take a look at my business and give me some ideas and tips and thoughts on what we could do to improve it."

I said, "Sure. What are you doing currently to market your business?" He said, "Well, we spend $3,000 a month on radio ads, we spend about $2,500 on print ads and we spend about $600 a month on these door hangers, which are almost like flyers that go on people's door handles."

I said, "How many people do you get in your store as a result of your radio ads?" There was silence. He had no idea. "How about your print ads?" Again, the same result. "OK, well, what about the door hangers?" He said, "That I do know."

I said, "Great, how many people do you get into your store as a result of your door hanger?" He said, "The last campaign that we did we got 21 people." I said, "How many door hangers did you get printed?" He said, "Ten thousand." So he spent $600 to get 10,000 door hangers printed and only 21 people came back into the store. That's roughly $30 per customer to get them into the store.

I said, "How much on average does each customer spend when they come into your store?" He said, "Around $15." You can see that he was losing $15 a customer to get those people in the store. What we then did was advised him to start building his email list.

So how does an offline store build their email list? Well, they set up a ballot box and each month he has a contest. People write their name and email on a ballot, they put it into the ballot box and each month he draws for a prize. Typically, it's like a pita party or something like that. At the same time he's building his list because those people are also entered into our preferred Pita Pick Club because the restaurant provides pitas.

Essentially now what happened is that he has built a list of just over 1,500 people and each month we do promotions for him and each month we generate significant sales that cost him nothing. I remember the first promotion we did for him, he called me back and said, "What did you just do? I can't believe it! We've generated more in our first hour than we have typically in our first day." He was extremely excited. That's the power of building a list.

You constantly want to focus on building a list and nourish that list and spend time with that list. Remember, those names are real people. You want to invest in those people by providing good value. If you just constantly bombard them with promotions and sell, sell, sell, and your focus is very self-centered, then you're not going to have the kind of conversions you could have if you focused on being of value to that list.

So number-one is realizing the value of list building but then the second part of that is understanding that it's a relationship process. You want to nourish that relationship by adding value to those people. You want to constantly be list building and focusing on building the relationship with that list.

3. **Knowing that the only way you will make sales is if you sell products and services on a regular basis.** It is tough for a lot of people, myself included, when you have to realize you have to send promotions at some point in time. Doesn't that contradict what I just said earlier where you don't want to bombard your list with promotions?

Yes and no. You want to continuously provide value so you want to provide tips and resources and give them good content, but at the same time you also want to send different promotions for different products and services. The most profitable are going to be promotions for your own products and services so that means you want to look to create your own products and you want to be continuously developing new products so that you can offer them to your list.

If you don't have your own products, start off by offering affiliate products; become an affiliate for other people's products that you know, like, or trust or have received value from yourself and continuously set up a schedule for mailing out your own promotions. The only way you can grow your business is if you continuously market and sell different and products and services to your particular list.

If you don't do it on a regular basis, then you're really going to be shooting yourself in the foot. So look to create a regular promotional schedule where you're sending out promotions on a regular basis.

4. Have long-term visions and goals. Many people are fly-by-night marketers where they don't know what they're doing this month and next month or even a year from now and as a result their business is very ad hoc, it's very sporadic. The way to build a successful long-term business is by having long-term goals.

Goal setting can sound flakey at times but if you don't know which direction you're headed, how can you ever get there? Even if you don't know it exactly, have some type of an idea of how you want to build your business, what you want your business looking like in one to five years from now and start moving in that direction.

HOW TO SET GOALS

— *"You want to take the big goal, break it down as much as possible, and then working on it from that point forward"*

Stanley: Speaking of setting goals, can you tell us the importance of goals? What's the process of setting goals?

Stu: Everybody's goals are going to be different based on their own interests and desires. As I mentioned, a lot of my interests are around the charity work that we're doing but it really depends on what you're looking to get out of your life. The more specific you can make them, the better. What I like to do is try to break them down into monthly goals.

If you're setting a big goal for the year, what does that mean on a monthly basis? If you starting out and you're looking to hit $100,000 in sales in your first year, what does that mean on a monthly basis? That means you're going to take the $100,000 and divide it by 12 and that's what your monthly goal is going to be.

What does that mean on a weekly basis? Take that number and divide it by four and that will give you your weekly goal. What does that mean on a daily basis? Again, take the weekly number and divide it by seven and that will give you your daily goal. Then it really boils down to much more manageable numbers.

Let's just take that example and say our goal is $100,000 a year in sales. We divide it by 12 months and that's going to give us roughly $8,333 a month that we need to generate. Divide that number by an average of 30 days and that means we need to generate $278 a day. Knowing that, what does that mean?

Then it really boils down to your numbers and your conversion rates. If your conversion rate is 3 percent and you're selling a $100 product, that means you need to sell about three a day and you need to get 100 people to that site per day. What do you need to do get 100 people to your site each day?

That's where it really goes, for me, is starting off with a big goal and breaking it down as much as possible because then it just becomes a system. It becomes much more manageable and much easier for you to tackle the goal. Just shouting out the goal and trying to go for it without knowing exactly what that means as to what you need to do on a daily basis in order to get there really becomes difficult.

You want to take the big goal, break it down as much as possible – I just gave you a quick example there – and then working on it from that point forward.

GET STARTED
— *"It's never too late to get started"*

Stanley: Stu, I have one last question for you. Can you name me one hero or role model who has influenced your life the most?

Stu: Wow, that's a real tough one for me, because I've been influenced by a lot of people. In the online world, definitely Armand Morin and Alex Mandossian have been huge influences on me, both in the way that they do business and in the way that they support the people who work with them and their JV partners and people on their staff.

They've been phenomenal individuals. They value their customers tremendously and they're always providing value. Those guys have been a huge influence on me, especially in my Internet marketing career.

Business wise, Richard Branson, for me, I had the pleasure of being able to meet him about a year ago and he's just an amazing guy. Here's a guy who at a very young age – I think he was 17 – when he started his first business and he's gone on to build a multi-billion dollar company.

He really lives his life the way that he wants to. He's a jetsetter, he does what he wants to do, he pursues the types of things he loves pursuing, and he's really a great example of somebody who has taken their business and used it as a platform to provide the kind of life and lifestyle that he wants and to make the kind of impact that he wants.

Another person who has influenced me is President Bill Clinton. I managed to see him three or four times and the presentation he gave, almost every single time, focused on the impact that we can have as private citizens on different people and on the world.

It was his speeches that really opened my eyes to the fact that here we are, everyday people, and yet knowing what we know, and using the resources that we have available to us, we can have an impact on people on the complete opposite side of the world. I think that's really changed my focus and the focus of my wife and my family because of a lot of what he said.

Then I'm a big sports fan so I have my sports heroes like Lance Armstrong. There's a guy who had everything stacked against him. He was on his deathbed and yet he found a way to battle back and not only battle back but win the Tour de France seven times in a row.

You talk about motivation and you talk about being in a situation where you just want to give up and don't want to move forward and then you look at Lance Armstrong and what he went through and it really reminds you of the fact that you can always go that little step further.

I have many people whom I look up to, many people who have influenced me and they've all influenced me in their own individual ways and as a result they've guided me through different obstacles in my life, different obstacles in my business, and challenges and I can't wait to see what happens as the years go by here.

Stanley: Stu, I want to thank you for your time. Are there any final comments you want to add? Do you want to let people know about your main website where they can get more information about you?

Stu: My final comments for everybody are that it's never too late to get started with your online business or if you're looking to pursue an offline business. Going into business for yourself, for me, is the greatest thing ever. Is it more responsibility? Yes. Does it take more work in the beginning? Yes.

But does it have the kind of rewards we all want? The answer there is absolutely yes. It provides you more flexibility, more freedom, the financial rewards are a lot greater, and the impact that you can have on not only your family but other people's lives is there as well. It's never too late and the great thing about the Internet is that it can happen so quickly.

It was just a few years ago that I started my affiliate management business and that whole thing just took off like wildfire based on the fact that we did a very good job, we provided tremendous value, and we were good at what we do.

When you have your customers' focus in mind, you're going to always be successful, because whether you're providing products and services or whether you're providing value in some other form, as long as you have your customers' best interests in mind, you're setting yourself up for success.

If people would like to learn more about me, then I highly recommend you definitely check out my blog which is at MyIdeaGuy.com/blog. That's basically the hub where people can go to find information about my other products and services and get great articles. I continuously add new articles and insights on that particular blog so they can freely go there and see those.

CHAPTER 9

JOEL CHRISTOPHER:
The Master List Builder

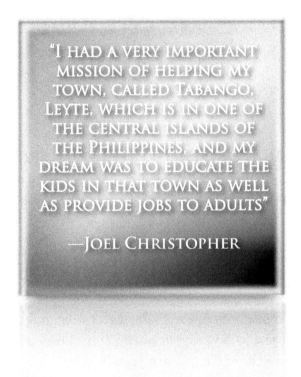

"I HAD A VERY IMPORTANT MISSION OF HELPING MY TOWN, CALLED TABANGO, LEYTE, WHICH IS IN ONE OF THE CENTRAL ISLANDS OF THE PHILIPPINES, AND MY DREAM WAS TO EDUCATE THE KIDS IN THAT TOWN AS WELL AS PROVIDE JOBS TO ADULTS"

—JOEL CHRISTOPHER

ON AUGUST 8, 1988, A YOUNG PHYSICAL THERAPIST FROM THE *Philippines by the name of Joel Christopher set foot in the United States with only $800 to his name. He was a techno-dummy who knew nothing about computers – his only mission was to have a better life for his family and hopefully one day return and retire in the Philippines.*

In 1999, he discovered the power of making money on the Internet, and launched his first website on January 1, 2000. He was just what they call a "newbie." But after a year of failing online, he figured out the key – the money is in the list. Two months later, he was able to quit his job and became a full-time Internet marketer.

Today, Joel is a best-selling author, speaker and mentor known worldwide as the Master List Builder. He has built and grown his own opt-in list to more than 200,000 subscribers and on the way to amassing that huge list there was one period when he tripled his list to over 30,903 in only 99 days.

Joel has attended more than 100 live seminars, bootcamps and conferences, and has spoken at more than half of them on the topic of list building. He has shared the stage with many marketing legends including Ted Nicholas, Joe Sugarman, Robert Allen, Mark Victor Hansen, Mark Joyner and many more.

FROM PHYSICAL THERAPIST TO INTERNET MARKETER

— *"My long-term goal was to go back to the Philippines, retire and help my town there and I also wanted to have a portable income. That's how I got started with the Internet"*

Stanley: Joel, can you tell us a bit about your background, starting from 1988 when you first went to America, and how you eventually discovered the Internet?

Joel: Sure. I am originally from the Philippines. I went to the U.S. on 8/8/88 with $800 to my name as a young, licensed physical therapist. I did that for about 13 years, traveled for the first five years, and had my own practice and home health agency the rest of the time. Health care in the U.S., especially in my niche, my area of physical therapy, went down hill in 1997 to 1998, so I had to close my practice, close my home health agency.

It had been very successful, but the market was not paying at the time because Medicare went down, which is the health care system in the U.S. for the older population. So I had to take a job in 1998, which was a hard thing to do, especially since I'd been my own boss. I'm sure some of you can relate.

I got married in April of 1999. My computer, which I never really touched, because my office manager always worked on it – I was really a techno-dummy at the time and didn't even have an email address – was in our third bedroom, which has been my office for the past eight years and I walked by one day and saw the computer just laying there gathering dust.

I said, "I heard that you can make money on the Internet." That was the time, around 1999, of the Internet Boom, if you'll recall. In fact, there was a term that was created based on what Marc Andreessen did with Netscape, called "instantaire," where young kids in their 20s or younger become millionaires and sometimes billionaires almost overnight.

I thought, "If I could get into this thing, that would be great." So I did some research. Actually, my long-term goal was to go back to the Philippines, retire and help my town there and I also wanted to have a portable income. That's how I got started with the Internet.

Stanley: What did you do in your early days as an Internet marketer?

Joel: I actually did a lot of reading and research for the first six months. If I had to do it again, I'd do something right away. It took me six months to analyze it and see if it was a good thing to do. On September 13, 1999, I bought a domain named SuccessAccess.com, which was my very first site. I launched it on January 1, 2000.

I had only 19 people on my list and in fact, most of them were relatives, friends and patients. I was still working as a full-time physical therapist at the time. I was an affiliate marketer for Internet marketing e-books for about a year and a half my first time. I got into the Master List Builder niche in May, 2001. So in the beginning, I was an affiliate marketer, selling other people's e-books and software for the most part.

BECOMING THE MASTER LIST BUILDER

— *"I didn't really come up with the name; my client George Callens did"*

Stanley: What led you to discover that the money is in the list?

Joel: That's a good question. It was a series of events. I went to an information marketing bootcamp with Dan Kennedy and Ron LeGrand, and they were talking about building a list because the money is in the list. I thought, "That's a good idea." Then one time, there was an interview being done in September of 2000 and five of the gurus at the time – including Terry Dean, Corey, Jonathan Mizel, Yanik Silver – were interviewed.

The question asked of them was, "What was your biggest mistake when you first got started online?" The common answer was that they didn't build a list or they didn't build the list big enough, soon enough. That was a realization.

So about two weeks after that, I did an email survey to my list (Marlon Sanders says you should survey your list) with one question, "What is your biggest problem right now?" The number-one answer from about 600 people who responded was they didn't know how to build a list from scratch. That's how the money is in the list – the Master List Builder system got started.

Stanley: What inspired you to come up with the Master List Builder?

Joel: It was really that one-question survey. I send a lot of surveys to my list and I just did an "Ask the Master List Builder" webinar, where I answered questions from my list members and I'll continue to do it in the next coming weeks. That was the thing that really got me started, although at the time, it wasn't known as the Master List Builder system.

I basically sent a survey, got responses, and the number-one answer to the question was how to build a list from scratch, so I went all over the place – through my hard drive and my bookshelves – and didn't find a system to build a list, so October 3, 2000, I made an announcement to my list and challenged myself.

I said, "I'm going to double my list of 10,000 to 20,000 in the remaining 90 days of this year." I went ahead with it, monitored my progress, I announced, about every week, how big my list was growing. In 74 days, it doubled to 20,548, so I had 16 days remaining in the year so I said, "Let me push it further."

In 99 days, on January 9, 2001, I was able to triple my list to 30,903. That's how the Master List Builder system got started, but again, it wasn't named that until February 24, 2002. I was interviewed by one of my clients, George Callens, who is now the chief operations officer for Armand Morin.

He was my first coaching client, and while introducing me, he said, "Joel Christopher is the 'Master List Builder' to whom Internet veterans go to help them build their lists." While he was talking, I was thinking, "That's a great name!" So I went to GoDaddy.com, typed in MasterListBuilder.com and it was available. The rest is history. So I didn't really come up with the name; my client George Callens did.

THE MASTER LIST BUILDER SYSTEM:
HOW TO TRIPLE YOUR LIST TO 30,903 IN 99 DAYS

— *"The biggest reason for the success was the drive, the challenge, the enthusiasm to make it happen"*

Stanley: What do you think was the biggest reason behind that success?

Joel: The biggest reason behind the success was:

1. **My drive to really make it happen.** I like challenges. I'm doing another challenge in the next 99 days starting December 1, at BuildYourList. com. This time, I'm challenging my list members to build their lists. I'm rewarding them to the tune of $10,000 in prizes and cash if they win. No one did that for me – I did it for myself.

2. **I was able to discover, and eventually create, a step-by-step system on how to build a list from scratch.** Because I have 12 weeks within the 90 days, I had to come up with something every week. I had five people who I was coaching for free at the time to help them build their lists and one of them was George Callens.

(You can learn more about Joel's system at MasterListBuilder.com)

BECOMING A BEST-SELLING AUTHOR
— *"We made it a best seller because of the lists that we've built and promoted the book to our list"*

Stanley: You are the best-selling author of the book *Mining Online Gold with an Offline Shovel*. What inspired you to write this book and how were you able to make it a best seller?

Joel: It was a client of mine, George McKenzie, who asked to co-author an e-book with me. I said, "I don't want an e-book, I want a print book." Just like you, Stanley, you're smart for thinking of a print book published with a major publisher, because it is more credible. So he gave me the idea, which is combining online list building with offline promotions, because he's a PR expert.

That inspired me and we basically got the book from concept to best seller in 93 days. The way we did it was really through my list and a lot of my joint venture partners' lists, like Mark Joyner, Mike Litman and Jason Oman. We made it a best-seller because of the lists that we've built and we promoted the book to our lists.

It became number-one in three categories, second only to the fifth Harry Potter book. We didn't know it was coming out that day – it was actually my 37th birthday on March 27, 2003.

THE MISSION OF THE MASTER

— *"I've got a few strong motivations: Number one, my dream of helping my town and, number two, my dream of really having this great lifestyle and great time with my kids and family"*

Stanley: What motivated you to carry on?

Joel: I had a very important mission of helping my town, called Tabango, Leyte which is in one of the central islands of the Philippines, and my dream was to educate the kids in that town as well as provide jobs to adults.

So I started a scholarship program in 1994 and my thought was to help one child a year; now my goal is to help 1,000 in the next three years and then provide them jobs through my company. So I'm actually building an outsourcing company in the Philippines.

This has been my dream as early as 1992 when I first wrote my mission statement. That kept me going despite all the obstacles, because you know that there are a lot of obstacles you have to get past in this business – I lost money in the beginning – and I held on to that dream and now it's becoming more and more of a reality.

My goal was to retire in my hometown by age 45, which is less than five years from now, and it looks like I'm going to be there sooner. I'll meet my dream of actually retiring and making a difference in that town by 2010. That was the main thing that kept me going.

The second thing, of course, was because I have a family – a wife and children – to feed. But beyond that, it was the time with them and the lifestyle, being able to see my kids grow, take my daughter to school, to piano lessons, to ballet lessons, take my son to swimming lessons and see them grow up.

So I've got a few strong motivations: Number one, my dream of helping my town and, number two, my dream of really having this great lifestyle and great time with my kids and family.

THE POWER OF JOINT VENTURES

— *"You really have to do your due diligence in finding out who you're going to partner with because I've had partners who stole from me"*

Stanley: Joel, if you could start all over again, what three things would you do differently?

Joel: Here are the three things I would have done:

1. Find a mentor right away

2. Outsource as soon as possible

3. Find partners all over the world as soon as possible and license my system

Stanley: What do you think is the biggest key to a successful joint venture partnership?

Joel: I believe there are two keys:

1. **Trust.** You really have to do your due diligence in finding out who you're going to partner with because I've had partners who stole from me. That was a big setback that I had in 2005 and it almost got me out of the business. I didn't do my due diligence. I trusted so much before this person even earned the trust.

2. **It's got to be a really big win for both,** not just a half-win for one and one-and a-half for the other; it's got to be an equal, win-win situation. Actually it should be a three-way win: A win for you, your partner and for the clients, who is really the biggest winner. I would get joint venture partners from people I already know, like and trust, especially if they're already in my client database.

I notice the ones who would really work well for me. For example, my very best partnership to this point was really with a guy named Chuck Daniel, who was my very first high-end, one-year mentoring client. He just got out of Microsoft three or four years ago and we've been partners for a few projects. He's somebody I really trust, I love him, and my daughter adores him because he's such a fun guy to be with.

MVP: MISSION, VISION, PASSION

— *"Do something that you really love to do. Turn a hobby into a business. Turn something you love to do that even if you don't get paid to do it, you'd still do it. That's the secret of success"*

Stanley: What advice would you give to a beginner in Internet marketing?

Joel: I have two advice:

1. Do not go into the Internet marketing niche and duke it out with these big gurus. Go and find another niche. There are a gazillion niches out there.

2. Make sure you know your mission. I call it MVP: Mission, Vision, Passion, meaning you go after what you're here for on this earth. What is your purpose? It's got to be more than just making money. Money is just a tool; that's not what we're here for. We're here to make a difference, we're here to build a family, we're here to build a community, whatever it is for you – what's your mission?

   Then find out what your long-term goals are and decide what you're going to do with your money. What are you going to do five, ten, or twenty years from now? Set the goal and set your vision.

Most importantly, find your passion. Do something that you really love to do. Turn a hobby into a business. Turn something you love to do that even if you don't get paid to do it, you'd still do it. That's the secret of success, to be able to do something you love. I love doing this – talking, meeting people, speaking, teaching – and even if I didn't get paid.

I did this when I was in college. I talked to kids in my class who were not as fast at getting information as I was able to and I enjoyed it although I didn't get paid to do it. I got a lot of dates from girls, but aside from that, there was no money for a payoff, but I enjoyed it. So find your passion. Turn your passion into your pension.

SUCCESS OF THE MASTER

— *"To me, success is what you leave — the mark, the name, the legacy — and what you've done on this earth while you're living"*

Stanley: How do you define success and do you think you have achieved that kind of success?

Joel: Success to me is being with my kids. To me, success is playing with my kids and being happy with my kids, like last Friday after Thanksgiving, we were out the whole day shopping. I was looking for a camera and my two kids were with me. My wife was shopping for clothes. I took them to Chuck E. Cheese. To me, every day is a success because I know my kids are taken care of and they're happy.

The second definition of success to me is doing something for somebody who is not able to repay you. For example, the very first scholar I had back in 1993 was a poor child who would not have made it through high school if I didn't send her to school. Now she's an accountant and is even the office manager of my office in Manila. She's attuned to my dream of building this community in our town because she was a part of that.

To me, that's something. Most importantly, I believe that it is not exactly what you get in your lifetime that's a true measure of success. It's not the cars, the house or the material possessions. To me, it's what you leave – the mark, the name, the legacy – and what you've done on this earth while you're living. Will you be remembered for it after you pass on? To me, that's the true measure of success.

FOCUS AND DELEGATION

– *"You've got to do what you do best and then delegate the rest. You can't do it alone; you've got to have a team"*

Stanley: How are you able to focus on one project at a time and not get distracted by other things?

Joel: I get distracted sometimes. I'm only human. However, I've developed this magnificent, almost obsessive focus since I was a kid. I learned good study habits as early as grade school. My IQ is just above average, however, despite that, I was able to rank number-one in high school and college and was valedictorian.

How could I do that? It was because of the drive and the focus. Also, I actually had a system as early as 12 or 13 years old. I already had a planner and planned my days and weeks, so I was able to balance my life. I had a girlfriend in my teens; I was class president; I was on the track team and the power lifting team in high school and college.

I was in extra-curriculars like choir, and I was number-one in class. How was I able to do all of that? I had a system. One system that I recommend in terms of time management is *The 7 Habits of Highly Effective People* by Stephen Covey. I follow his system of weekly planning. That's how I was able to focus.

Again, focus on your mission. If you live your day knowing that you have a mission on this earth and your time is limited, there is a sense of scarcity that, "I may not live to tomorrow. I've got to do the best I can today." That's why I have this amazing focus on what I do.

Another thing – delegation. You've got to do what you do best and then delegate the rest. You can't do it alone; you've got to have a team.

Stanley: As Robert Kiyosaki said, "Business is a team sport."

Joel: Absolutely!

THE MASTERY MINDSET AND BELIEF SYSTEM

— *"The mindset must be that of a master. I call it the mastery mindset. You do one thing, you master it"*

Stanley: In your opinion, what mindset and belief should one have to succeed in Internet marketing?

Joel: The mindset must be that of a master. I call it The Mastery Mindset. I teach this in the very first session of my Master List Builder Funshop, meaning you're not just a dabbler or a junkie. You do one thing, you master it. That's the mindset. The belief system is:

1. It's possible for you to succeed

2. It's possible that you can do it

3. You're able to succeed, not just because of what you get materially, but what you can give to others and the effect you have

     It's more of an abundance mentality belief that there's a lot of everyone on this earth and you have a God-given gift of making it. Hanging around with the right people is important as well as listening to audios, CDs and mp3s that tell you that you can do it. Of course reading books would help too.

Stanley: Joel, I want to thank you for sharing your story with us. I really appreciate it. Where can people go to get more information about you?

Joel: My pleasure! You can visit my blog over at MasterListBuilder.com for more details on my Master List Builder system of how you can triple your leads, sales and profits. If you want to find out more about my Master List Builder Funshop, you can go to MasterListBuilderFunshop.com.

CHAPTER 10

JASON JAMES:
Internet Millionaire and Product Launch Expert

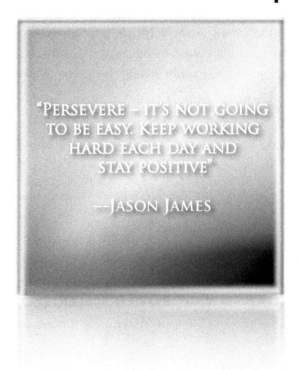

"PERSEVERE —IT'S NOT GOING TO BE EASY. KEEP WORKING HARD EACH DAY AND STAY POSITIVE"

—JASON JAMES

JASON JAMES HIT ROCK BOTTOM.

Labeled as a screw up in high school and forced to drop out of college...had four maxed out credit cards with daily harassment calls from bill collectors... watched helplessly as his brand new sports car was being repossessed...forced to live with his parents in his late 20's.

Things couldn't get any worse...everything went wrong, over and over again. His life got really bad. He was a mess and "A-Lost-Cause" for ever striking it rich.

Then it went from bad to worse.

He got fired from his job when he needed it the most and his girlfriend of three years dumped him...in his own words he had "the worst attitude anybody could possibly have."

For Jason, it was the end. Broke, lost, heartbroken and hopeless, Jason was down and out and had no idea what to do next...

But he changed his life around.

Now he's a highly accomplished and sought-after speaker; a top-gun consultant with expertise in eBay marketing, membership websites, Internet marketing, joint ventures, product launches, motivational tactics and strategic planning.

He has had five six-figure product launches and his company has achieved over $2.5 million in sales in the past two years. He has been to over 20 Internet marketing seminars and has worked with some of the top Internet marketing gurus.

So what happened? What turned it around?

FROM FLAT BROKE TO EBAY POWER SELLER

— *"In high school, I was a troublemaker and barely graduated — I got straight Ds"*

Stanley: Jason, let's start off by discussing the difficulties you faced in high school and how you managed to overcome them.

Jason: In high school, I was not your model student, if you will. I was a troublemaker; I didn't show up for class. I barely graduated. I had to go to summer school just to graduate from high school; I got straight Ds. After high school, I wasted time hanging out with friends and girls, and having a business and getting my life together was not a priority at all.

So I just wasted about for a few years during and after high school, and then I was lucky enough to make the decision to go into the military.

Stanley: What was life like in the military and how did it eventually lead you to your Internet marketing career?

Jason: Life in the military was OK. It was difficult. The day-to-day stuff is probably the hardest. It's great to be in the military to serve your country, but when you're waking up every morning at 5am to go run five miles day after day, it's kind of a grind. But overall, it was a great experience and I also got started in business while I was in the military.

When you enlist in the military here in the U.S., they don't pay you very well. You get a place to stay and you get food, but the base pay is pretty poor, so I started selling some stuff on eBay to supplement my income. In the military, people are always coming and going – on deployment, overseas, changing duty stations.

I don't know if this is just a military thing, but young guys like to "pimp out" their rooms and have these big-screen TVs, a big stereo, the fancy gaming systems, DVD players etc. Obviously if they were deployed overseas, they couldn't take that stuff with them, so they would come to me and say, "Can you sell this stuff on eBay?"

I said, "Sure." So I would take people's stuff, sell it on eBay and they'd give me a percentage of the sale, usually around 10 percent. That was my first taste of an actual business. I was in the military for four years and decided it was great experience and got started a little bit in the eBay thing.

Stanley: You actually became an eBay power seller. Tell us a bit about that.

Jason: I did, actually. When I got out of the military in 2004, I didn't want a job – that I knew. I didn't want to have a boss. I was always an entrepreneur at heart, so I started selling on eBay full time and, within three months, I became a power seller. I was selling electronics, like I had done in the military.

I realized that on eBay, while it's great for part-time income, to run it as a full-time business, it's very labor intensive. There's a lot of work that goes into it with shipping, customer service and auction listings, and there's a bit of a ceiling on how much you can earn. I sold on eBay as a power seller for a good six months and was probably making, in gross sales, about $10,000 to $15,000 a month.

I decided I was really good at it. I had a formula on how to make money, so why didn't I create a product on how to sell on eBay? The product put itself together, really. All the time I had been selling on eBay, I discovered the wholesalers where people could go and get products to sell, the best auction listing templates to use to get the most bids.

I learned tips and secrets to sell on eBay, little things that make items sell every time. These were all scattered about on my computer so I put all these things together, as e-books, articles, tips, secrets and wholesalers, into a membership website, which turned out to be my first product called Auction Resource Network and it sells to this day.

Over a few months' time, I discovered what a JV partner was, so I asked people to promote it. I said, "I'll give you 50 percent of the sales if you promote this for me." So it wasn't really a launch – I put it out there and then tried to promote it as much as I could – but it was my first product. And in the first year, I did $246,000 in sales.

HOW TO RECRUIT JV PARTNERS...
EVEN IF YOU ARE A NEWBIE
— *"The key is to find targeted people"*

Stanley: How were you able to get JV partners to promote your site?

Jason: When you're first starting out, it's very difficult because people haven't heard of you, they don't know how good the product is, and I hadn't met a lot of these people. Now, at the point I'm at in my marketing career, I know a lot of people. I've been to over 20 seminars and have met a lot of people face to face.

I've promoted stuff for other people, but when you're first starting out, there's no way you can promote stuff for other people because you don't have a mailing list. There's no way you can get to seminars because you haven't come up yet or you don't have the money to get to them, because they can be expensive.

Just starting out, you have to contact as many people as possible. If you contact 100 people, odds are, maybe five people will promote for you, but that's enough to get you started, make some money and get your name out there. If you had one person promote and they had a 5 percent conversion rate and made $2,000, you can then contact other people who don't know about you and use those numbers to say, "This person promoted. Here's what they did. They did great, so I think you should promote."

The key is to find targeted people. I had an eBay product, so I found people who have other eBay products. They had mailing lists and eBay-related services. I contacted all these people who were in the eBay business niche and gave them a free copy of the product.

I said, "I'll give you X amount in commission per sale. Will you promote for me?" Most people either didn't reply or said no, but there were a few who did reply and promoted for me, and the rest is history, because once you get started like that, there's a snowball effect.

HOME RUN! FIRST BIG SUCCESS
— *"It doesn't seem real, but it did happen and it's pretty amazing"*

Stanley: A year later, in July 2006, you came up with a product called Uncut Marketing. What was that about and what inspired you to create that product?

Jason: The eBay product was going great and I wanted a way to supplement my income. At that time, I had been to a few seminars and met some people, so I got an idea to interview the people I had met and the JV partners who promoted Auction Resource Network. I thought, "Why don't I contact those people and interview them?" like you're interviewing me now, Stanley.

I asked them if they'd get on the phone with me for 30 minutes or an hour so I could ask their success secrets, what they did when they were struggling and that type of stuff. What turned out was a product called Uncut Marketing, which was 20 interviews with some of the top marketers in the Internet marketing arena. I charged $97 for that product.

In the first two weeks alone, I had just over $200,000 in sales, so it did really, really well. I took an entire year to make $246,000 with Auction Resource Network, but this product did over $200,000 in the first two weeks.

When you see that kind of money come in, it doesn't seem real. It seems fake or like it's not really happening, but it did happen and it's pretty amazing. That was back in July 2006. So that was my first huge success.

THE SECRET TACTIC BEHIND THE $300,000 LAUNCH

— *"The money is in the backend"*

Stanley: What was your next product?

Jason: I believe that was Membership Riches, at MemberRiches.com. My first two products were both membership websites, where you had to get a username and password to sign up, so I decided to put a product together that talked about how a beginner could get started with their own membership website, what script to use to manage the members, how to take payments, how to get content for your member's area etc.

This was my biggest product launch which did $319,000 in the first two weeks. To this day, I haven't beaten that number, but I was pretty happy with that, to say the least, for the first two weeks of the product launch to do over $300,000.

Stanley: Membership Riches was your most successful product launch to date. What do you think was the main reason behind this success?

Jason: It was a combination of JV partners and the product itself. I had an upsell, where after they bought the $97 Membership Riches e-book, I sold a product for $4,000, which was a membership website that was already built. It had the content, the sales letter, and everything was done for them – it was pretty much a membership website in a box.

People bought an e-book on how to start a membership website, but immediately they were forwarded to an offer where it said, "Stop for a second. We already built this membership website for you. If you're interested, here you go. It's $4,000." I made about 55 sales of that product, so that was a huge part of the success, having that upsell or backend.

Stanley: The money is in the backend.

Jason: Yes, very much so.

Stanley: What was your next product?

Jason: My next product was Audio Video Riches, at AVRiches.com. As you'll see, each product I do is built on previous successes. For example, I had started two membership websites, so I did a product on how to do a membership website. All of my launches before that had all incorporated some sort of video or audio, whether it was video to recruit JV partners or audio on the sales letter.

I had learned a lot about putting audio and video on the Internet, so I created Audio Video Riches, which is a beginner's guide to creating, producing and uploading Internet audio and video. Using audio and video in my previous product launches had increased sales and conversions, so I made this product. That product launched March 15, 2007, and did $114,000 in the first two weeks.

LEVERAGE YOUR JV PARTNER'S TRAFFIC

— *"I took advantage of the huge amount of traffic from my JV partners by being aggressive about where I put the opt-in boxes, using a pop-in window"*

Stanley: Throughout all those product launch successes, were you able to leverage your JV partners' traffic and build yourself a big list?

Jason: Absolutely. There are several ways that I built my list. There's article marketing and forum posting, for example. But the biggest way is when I launched a product, on my sales letter I would have a drop-in box, an HTML form, where I would give away a free report; "If you're unsure about this product, click here for the first three chapters free." That type of thing.

I would collect as many subscribers as I could. There was also a huge amount of traffic coming to the site from my JV partners so I would take advantage of that traffic by being aggressive about where I put the opt-in boxes, using a pop-in window, and to date my list is just under 80,000 people.

Stanley: After building yourself a list, did you start promoting other people's products and becoming a super affiliate?

Jason: Absolutely. One of my major sources of income is affiliate marketing. You see these products launching all the time that have contests and cash prizes, real high-ticket stuff. With every major product launch that comes out, I try to make the top ten of each launch. Affiliate marketing is a big part of what I do, and a lot of that had to do with utilizing my mailing list. I mail out to my mailing list about the latest and greatest products, but I still do my own product development as well.

Stanley: What are some affiliate marketing tactics you use to get yourself into the top ranking for affiliate competitions? Do you offer bonuses?

Jason: Yes, absolutely. With the concept of bonuses, originally, I thought, "Shouldn't the product itself be enough?" If you're interested in a product on, "How to use Google AdWords," shouldn't that product be enough? But for some reason, if you, as an affiliate marketer, add an extra bonus, something really valuable, people will buy through your link.

I think using a unique bonus, something you haven't offered before, can definitely get you more sales, and get you listed higher up in the affiliate competitions. So I think bonuses are very important to affiliate promotions because people, for some reason, want that extra bonus.

Subscribers of mine have told me that they've shopped around to all the different Internet marketers to see who has the best bonus – and that person will get the most sales.

A UNIQUE TACTIC THAT GENERATED AN EXTRA 100 SALES IN TWO DAYS

– *"To increase sales, give everyone who purchases access to all of your previous products"*

Stanley: What was your next product?

Jason: My next product was Untold Marketing Secrets, at TheUntoldSecrets.com, which was very similar to my first major success, Uncut Marketing. It's pretty much the same type of product with a little twist. I interviewed over 20 elite marketers – the most successful people I could find – and asked them, "What are your top secrets to success? I don't want you to tell me what you tell everyone; I want you to dig deep in your brain and tell me your top success secrets. Don't hold anything back." Hence the name Untold Marketing Secrets. I asked them what's been most important in their success and, once again, I put this in a membership site.

That launched just a few months ago and it ended up doing $104,000 in sales. Once again, it was a six-figure product launch with expert interviews. There's a market for that. People want to learn from other people's failures and successes, so that was another big success for me.

Stanley: When you launched Untold Marketing Secrets, you offered a bonus where anybody who purchased it would get all of your previous products for free. Is that correct?

Jason: That's correct. A friend of mine suggested, to increase sales, why not give everyone who signs up access to all of your previous products? I did just under 1,000 sales for the product itself, but after sending that email telling people that if they signed up they'd get access to all of my previous products, it resulted in an immediate surge of over 100 additional sales in two days. That tactic alone was worth thousands of dollars for me.

Stanley: Did you think you might have put-off some of your previous, loyal customers who purchased from you in the past, who might have spent $300 to get all of your products, and somebody else just comes in and gets them for only $47?

Jason: I did think about that, and it was a chance I took. People were still paying for these products; they weren't available for free. It's a chance I took and it worked out. I didn't get any emails or contacts from people who were upset about it, saying they wanted their money back from purchasing my previous products. I didn't get any negative feedback on it, and it worked out.

Stanley: This is a really, really powerful product launch technique. By making the offer absolutely irresistible, you've really pushed up the sales and I think people should try this tactic out.

Jason: Yes, definitely. Like I said, it created an immediate surge in sales. Also, I told my JV partners, "When you email your subscribers, tell them that when they sign up, they'll get access to all of my previous products." So it was, once again, a snowball effect. This would give people a reason to send this out to their mailing lists, and it created more sales for me.

Stanley: What are some of your future projects?

Jason: Right now I'm doing a giveaway called GreedyGiveaway.com, which is where people sign up to get all these free gifts and the point of it is to build a list. With this giveaway, I'm going to try and get my list up over 100,000 subscribers, so my goal is to add another 20,000 subscribers. Once that's accomplished, through affiliate marketing, I can market to those leads over the next few months or year and leverage the giveaway success into big profit.

Building my list is one of the most important things I do in my business, so I think with a list of over 100,000 people, my affiliate marketing efforts will definitely improve. I'll make more money and get better results in the contests. It will allow me to work less while making more, which is probably the goal of most people.

UPDATE: *Although he did not reach his goal, Jason did go on to add over 11,038 subscribers to his mailing list in 10 days.*

CREATE A TO-DO LIST FOR EACH DAY
— *"Once you work hard day by day, your results will get greater and greater"*

Stanley: Jason, that was quite an inspirational story and just proves what an amazing business we're in. The Internet has transformed the lives of many. I just want to ask you, throughout your product launch success, what motivated you to continue?

Jason: People reading this may think that it was all great and everything worked out perfectly with no issues or doubts, but that's not true. There were times, before the six-figure product launches, when I was putting products together and seeds of doubt crept into my mind.

I thought, "Would anybody promote this? Would people buy it? Would it convert? Are people interested in this? Maybe I should just go back to college. This isn't for me." At the end of the day, what I did, and what I think people should do, is just make a list of what you want to accomplish each day, take each day and keep working hard, keep persevering, and I think people will be OK.

Stanley: Do you mean people should create a to-do list for each day?

Jason: Yes, create a to-do list for each day. I think that's very important. Do it the night before. Once you accomplish your to-do list for the day, go out and have fun. That night, create another to-do list for the next day. Once you have that list done, go out and have fun, go to the beach, take a day trip somewhere. Once you get the most important things done, go have some fun.

Then once the next day comes, it's all business. Once you get business done, have some fun. Once you work hard day by day, your results will get greater and greater because sometimes people have problems actually getting things done and they're confused on what they need to do.

If you put a simple, easy to-do list together each night before you go to bed on what you need to get done for the next day, over time, you'll see that you will get so much more done, as opposed to just waking up in the morning and saying, "Oh, what should I do today? I don't know, maybe I'll do this," and wasting so much time.

A lot of people fall into this cycle, where they just wake up and they don't know what they want to accomplish or what their goals are – they don't know anything. If you put down what you want to accomplish on paper, you'll get so much more done and you'll make more money in the end.

THE 3 MAIN INGREDIENTS TO MARKETING SUCCESS
— *"You don't have to get it right, you just have to get it going" (Mike Litman)*

Stanley: In your opinion, what are the three main ingredients to success as an Internet marketer?

Jason: I would say:

1. **Build your list** – the money is definitely in the list. I would build my list from day one, which is something I didn't do. Once I started in eBay after I got out of the military, I wish I had started building my list, which I didn't start doing until a year after that when I launched my first product. I missed an entire year to build it.

   For those just starting out, get an autoresponder and start building your mailing list. It's so important to be able to communicate with your customers and prospects, so build your list early and often.

2. **Treat your customers like gold,** because once you have a customer who has sent you their own, hard-earned money and you treat them like gold, they'll be more than likely to purchase from you again.

   Before, when I was frustrated and things weren't going the way I'd like, people would email me and I'd just delete the email or I would reply with an attitude saying, "No, you can't have a refund." Or, "You're a scammer. Leave me alone." I let my frustration get the best of me and I would treat paying customers rudely, which is completely unacceptable.

   So now I try and treat every customer, even if they're angry or have a problem, with respect and give them the benefit of the doubt. The customer is always right, so do everything in your power to make the customer happy because once you have a happy customer, they'll tell their friends about you and buy from you again so it's a win-win.

3. **Work hard but remember to have fun along the way** because life is short. Leave time for family or your pets or your passions – whatever you want to do.

   When I was first starting out, I would be in front of the computer for 16 hours a day. I'd have bags under my eyes, I wouldn't get out of the house, I wouldn't shave and I'd just be a bum. Now, I only work a few hours a day. I take care of myself, I exercise, I spend a lot of time with my family. So work hard but remember to have fun.

Stanley: What advice would you give to a beginner who is just starting out in Internet marketing?

Jason: The best piece of advice I can give to people just starting out is when you're creating a product or your business initially, you're going to want everything to be perfect, but don't do that. Just create a product, get it out there, get it seen by people, get feedback on it, and then build from there.

The hardest thing is to put yourself out there and be vulnerable. But put it out there, put it up for sale, give free copies to JV partners and see what they think, get feedback on it, and just use it to build like building blocks. Take all the feedback you receive and then make it better and better. Don't just sit there and work on something for six months just to make it perfect.

It's better and more effective to put it together as fast as you can and put it out there and see what people think about it, as opposed to just keeping it on your computer. That's the wrong approach, in my opinion. Persevere – it's not going to be easy. Keep working hard each day and stay positive. Keep in mind that things will work out if you keep working hard, and good luck to people.

Stanley: Just like what Mike Litman said, "You don't have to get it right, you just have to get it going."

Jason: Exactly. That summarizes all that stuff I said, in one sentence.

Stanley: Jason, I want to thank you for being here. Is there anything else you'd like to add? Where can people find out more information about you?

Jason: Stanley, thank you for having me. I really appreciate it. My final advice is to remember to work hard, have fun, and good luck to everyone. If people want to learn more about me, they can go to TheRealIM.com.

CHAPTER 11

ROB COWIE:
President of Worldwide Brands, Inc.

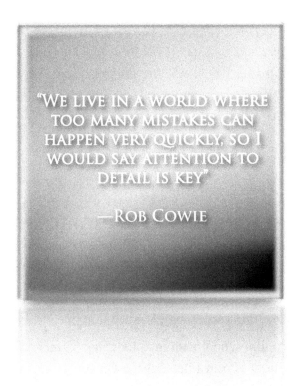

"WE LIVE IN A WORLD WHERE TOO MANY MISTAKES CAN HAPPEN VERY QUICKLY, SO I WOULD SAY ATTENTION TO DETAIL IS KEY"

—ROB COWIE

PRODUCING A CULT CLASSIC BLOCKBUSTER FILM MAY BE YOUR *average college film maker's dream, but it is one that became reality for Rob Cowie and his Haxan Five team.*

The release of The Blair Witch Project on July 16, 1999 rocked the movie industry. With a budget of only $25,000 and a ground-breaking Internet promo-

tional campaign, the film was a huge success and went on to gross over $248 million worldwide.

And that's only the beginning...

Later, Rob went on to pursue his dream of becoming an Internet entrepreneur and became the President of Worldwide Brands, the Internet's leading authority on product sourcing for home eBiz.

Rob is also the producer of the feature film Altered and the Fox TV Series FreakyLinks. His latest project is a film called Seventh Moon, which is currently being shot in Hong Kong.

Living in Hong Kong myself, I got the opportunity to talk to Rob one-on-one while he was there, and got him to share with us his aspiring story, including the multi-million dollar success of The Blair Witch Project, and his amazing accomplishment of taking Worldwide Brands from a customer base of 10,000 to over 150,000 active Internet entrepreneur members, with annual revenue in excess of $6 million dollars.

THE BEHIND THE SCENES OF THE BLAIR WITCH PROJECT

— *"They put him in this kind of prison camp to basically simulate the idea of being tortured and they submitted him to a barrage of things, short of actually really hurting him"*

Stanley: I understand that you actually studied film in college, is that right?

Rob: Yes. I went to film school with my producing partner and directing partner that I work with at Haxan Films, at the University of Central Florida in Orlando, Florida in United States.

Stanley: What was it like and how did it eventually lead you to The Blair Witch Project?

Rob: One of the greatest things about UCF was it was a brand new school and they had a bunch of equipment. Disney had just built a whole back lot and Universal had just built a back lot, so there were a lot of productions going on in town at the time. One of the greatest things about film school was that we really had free reign to go out to do anything we wanted to try.

We did 19 films together in film school. Ed (director of The Blair Witch Project) actually directed his first feature at film school and I produced a short film, which was about 30 minutes long, that I raised almost a million dollars to do. So it was just a really productive time and we were very fortunate not to hold back and just go for it.

Stanley: Who actually came up with the idea to do The Blair Witch Project and what was the experience like?

Rob: The Blair Witch Project originally was that the two guys who directed the movie, Dan Myrick and Eduardo Sanchez, had been talking about a film idea when we were in film school together and they had called that The Woods Project. Basically, it was a movie that was supposed to actually take place in the 70's and we were going to shoot it traditionally and it was all going to take place – we were going to be camping in the woods etc.

But later my producing partner Gregg Hale, who had been in the military; had done a bunch of military intelligence training. One of the things they did to him was they put him in this kind of prison camp to basically simulate the idea of being tortured and they submitted him to a barrage of things, short of actually really hurting him. They shorted food and they kept him captured and did all kinds of things like that. And it was Gregg who had the idea of applying that kind of technique to the actor and said, "Hey, wouldn't this be fun to do to actors?"

So the combination of both the original idea and then what Gregg had done, it was kind of a spark that started the whole process.

Stanley: So the film actually started out as just as an experiment?

Rob: Well, there were two parts to it:

The original idea was actually like this fairly normal narrative, but then it developed into this kind of being a real experiment. We shot the film real-time for 24 hours a day for eight days and that was kind of the experimental part of it, you know, the actors, she had the camera, we navigated them around by giving them GPS's and they had to hit all these different coordinates.

Then the other part was kind of a more traditional part. It was kind of a fake documentary. What happened is the experiment ended up working really well, way beyond what we had hoped. So the additional material – the documentary material – we ended up using as material for the website and material for the sci-fi special that ran on the sci-fi channel. It became book material and we even had a traveling museum. So right from the very early days, we had kind of a really rich content experience for people to engage in all the marketing and outlets.

HOW TO PROMOTE FILMS VIA THE INTERNET... AND MAKE $248 MILLION!

— *"It needs to be engaging, it needs to be back up, something people can explore into and something that people can really interact with"*

Stanley: The Blair Witch Project went on to generate over $248 million and you did this by promoting it through the Internet and creating a huge buzz. How did you do that?

Rob: It was the common samplings and a combination of promotional media. But definitely the thing that we were doing that at the time that not many other people were really doing was centering our audience's experience on the website. Very early on, BlairWitch.com kind of became the anchor for how we would leak out content, and it was really a byproduct of the two parts of the content because we had this really rich content and we presented it to the people. We just basically were putting enough there so people could explore it.

We did it in a way that I think was fun. For example, we have Heather's Journal: We put up the cover one day and then the next page in the journal will be somewhere on the site but you'll have to find it in the hidden link. Then we started making puzzles and that. We always tried to be very personable and very straight forward in how we were communicating to our fans and we still do that today on everything that we do.

You go to Haxan.com right now, we've got a pretty detailed blog that is covering day-by-day what we are shooting. I post on there, Ed, the director, posts on there and we just play really straight-forward; we play it really straight and tell everybody exactly what's going on and try and engage people. We've got a forum and this Sunday, actually, we're going to be doing some live chat with people where they can see the ten year anniversary of The Blair Witch Project.

So we always tried to engage people in the whole experience of the film and provide a really rich story experience for them, not only on Blair but on the TV shows we've did, on the film we did last year and another film that we're doing now. We're just trying really to involve our audience in the experience as much as we can.

Stanley: So you try to make the website interactive in a way?

Rob: Yeah, it needs to be engaging, it needs to be back up, something people can explore and something that people can really interact with. The great thing about the web is you really can have feedback both ways, so we try to really listen to our fans. We've got people who have followed us for ten years now; we really treasure that loyalty and that support.

WORLDWIDE BRANDS: GROWING A ONE-MAN OPERATION INTO A $6 MILLION SUCCESS

— *"We found a real problem that people were having, and we solved it and went beyond their expectations of what they wanted"*

Stanley: So was that your first taste of marketing through the Internet?

Rob: Yeah. I had done some early stuff just before Blair, but Blair was really the first time that we engaged on the Internet on a large scale. I had always been interested in it. But everybody was amazed at how strong a feedback there was.

Once Blair hid, we got involved in a bunch of other web-type things. I launched a company called PlanetOutdoors.com and did their whole website and commercials and branding and everything like that. We've done some consulting for a couple other companies that way.

The more we got engaged in the Internet and various different factors, the more I realized, as a producer, that really the future – and it's on, it is now, but more and more so in the future – direct marketing to your audience, target marketing to your audience would become increasingly more and more important. That was when I started getting the idea of going into something like Worldwide Brands where I could learn about that world of direct marketing and Internet commerce.

Stanley: You mentioned Worldwide Brands. Can you discuss a bit about that?

Rob: After Blair and the two TV shows, I was pretty burned out. We all were. We all decided, look, "We'll take off for a year and go our different ways." I traveled some and took some time off.

I wanted to have my own business that I could essentially take anywhere I wanted to be. It would provide me with income that I could then take and invest into different projects. I really didn't want to move to Los Angeles and work within that system because there were a lot of challenges, and my family was really established in Orlando. I did want to have something that I could travel with, and again, I was very interested in getting to understand how Internet marketing and Internet commerce survive and work.

So, I had found a guy who had started a business literally out of his garage, and that was Chris Malta. It was a very impressive little company. It was generating some good revenue but he really didn't know how to grow it from his one-man operation.

So, I said that I would help him do that and invest some money. I joined him, and together he and I grew the company over the next five years from that one-person operation to, really, this year it's going to be a $6 million dollar company.

It's been really terrific. The greatest thing that I have gotten out of Worldwide Brands is that we engage and help people all around the world succeed in online commerce. That has been a very personally gratifying experience because there's nothing like seeing fellow entrepreneurs succeed. It's a wonderful feeling.

Stanley: What is Worldwide Brands?

Rob: Worldwide Brands helps people, who sell online, find products that they can sell. For example, if you had an eBay store where you sell on eBay, at first you might start with things that you find in your attic or your basement, but sooner or later you're going to run out of those products. You need a supply for real products that you can buy at wholesale price and then turn around and sell that online.

Often times, e-commerce entrepreneurs, maybe it's a second job or maybe they don't have a lot of money to invest in sourcing. So they're kind of geographically challenged and a lot of them have to work out of their home.

So what we do is we actually find, qualify, and make sure that they're real suppliers who will supply products to those online retailers. We have a database that has almost nine million products now. We add multiple, multiple suppliers every day.

You pay a one-time fee to access our database and then you can literally put whatever product you're looking for, for example, shoes, TVs, flashlights, whatever. You put it in our search bar and it brings up suppliers. It gives you the contact name, it gives you the products that they carry, it gives you a bunch of detailed information on those suppliers, and they are guaranteed to work with you as an e-commerce retailer.

Stanley: From my understanding, there's actually this bar that you have incorporated into your database that gives you analysis of whether the product has a good chance of becoming successful. Tell us a bit about that.

Rob: Actually, that's a really good question because there are two main questions that you have to ask yourself as an online entrepreneur:

1. What should I sell?
2. Where can I find a supplier for that product?

The "What should I sell?" question is really important because there are different demands for products, and there are different suppliers for products. So there's different demand and different competition so you need to figure out what's the best product you can sell for the best price for the most profit.

Now, we built in an online research tool into our database as well, so not only can you actually find the suppliers but we give you the data that you need in order to make that decision on what to sell.

So we tell you, "Look, for this product, here's what the competition on the Internet is like right now, here's what the demand is like, here's the cost to advertise in these different places, this is what's going on in the eBay marketplace in these different places."

So really, the product that we have that Worldwide Brands makes is called One Source. It's just a very valuable tool because, as an e-commerce merchant, it cuts the amount of time that you have to spend in figuring all of that down to literally hours, where it could take weeks and months without us.

We're very grateful that it's been such a success as a product. We've got well over 150,000 companies now that use our tool. We grow every day and we work hard to keep the quality of the information at a real high level.

Stanley: What do you think is the main reason behind the success of Worldwide Brands?

Rob: I think that the main reason for the success of Worldwide Brands is the fact that it really solves a real-world problem that people have. We were able to identify that problem and then really create a tool that works. It's now been almost seven years that Worldwide Brands has been in business and, if it didn't solve people's problems for them, we would have never grown and we would have never done that.

Then we've continually focused on listening to our customers, getting feedback from them on what their problems are and then trying to improve our tool set to help people succeed.

Consequently, we have wonderful success stories that are part of our family and all that. But really, at its simplest point, we found a real problem that people were having and we solved it and went beyond their expectations of what they wanted.

That same idea is related to successful e-commerce. Some of my most successful e-commerce clients, what they do is find this normally very targeted niche, something that you can't go around the corner and buy at your big mall or your superstore. You can't get it very easily. You have to go online.

It's a little specialty product and it helps solve that problem for that customer. I think that's the future of commerce, essentially putting more and more of the things that people want at their fingertips.

GIVING BACK

— *"Content is king"*

Stanley: Moving on, what did you do next? Did you host your own radio show?

Rob: Yeah. We've always believed in education and information. Going back to The Blair Witch Project kind of lesson and also the successful websites we've had related to our other entertainment products, content is king. People have a huge desire to know how to do this.

E-commerce is challenging, and a lot of people are essentially starting from scratch. They're just starting at the beginning and they've got a huge need for education. So we provide a lot of information for free – a lot of really high quality education for free.

We built a little TV station in our office so we do video content that we produce that teaches people how to sell products online. We did a radio show – that was sponsored by Entrepreneur magazine. We write articles. We have blogs.

We continually try and focus on answering the questions that our customers have. So, the content is at the center of our website. It's a very deep website. It's got many, many, many, many pages and it really is a rich experience for people who engage at that web site.

Stanley: Just to remind everybody, what's the website URL again?

Rob: http://www.TheWorldwideBrands.com

Stanley: Excellent. What are some of your current and future projects?

Rob: I am now currently working on this movie called Seventh Moon and, if you go to Haxan.com, you can follow along on the blog. Or if you go to SeventhMoon.com you can follow along there too. So, Seventh Moon is my new movie project. I'm still working with Worldwide Brands.

I've got a number of other projects in the works. I'm actually going to do some family entertainment. I've written a couple of family scripts and then, after Seventh Moon I have some other movies that I'm going to do.

As always, Worldwide Brands, just like I tried to do from the beginning, it's wonderful that if I'm here in Hong Kong, I can follow along exactly what's going on with the company no matter what. My staff is actually spread out across the United States in various different places.

Look, we live in a wonderful time. We live in a wonderful age where people around the world can connect, interact, build things together and I'm just excited about being a part of that and kind of developing both the e-commerce world that I'm engaged in and then the entertainment world that I'm engaged in.

Every day, those worlds become closer and closer. It is not going to be too far off when your TV set on your wall, and really it is, already, but it's going to be more and more, exactly the same thing as your browser and you go and get exactly the kind of content that you want. So, what I had set out to do as far as going to school to learn how that works on the Internet by doing Worldwide Brands, has really paid off in the way that I approach doing all my entertainment and all my business.

TREAT YOUR BUSINESS SERIOUSLY

— *"One of the things that I would advise, especially to young entrepreneurs, is that they need to treat their business very, very seriously from a legal and financial and accounting point of view"*

Stanley: Rob, that's quite a story. Like all Internet entrepreneurs, it's not always been a smooth journey. What failures or mistakes have you made in the past, and what lessons did you learn from them?

Rob: Oh, absolutely. If I could give one piece of advice that I think has paid off for me very well, is that you should test and try everything. I have put out so many different ideas or start-ups. It's so to create a website very quickly or do multiple versions of websites. We do a lot of split testing when we are engaged in Worldwide Brands. We do a lot of trials of ideas.

It's the same thing with the entertainment world. If Hollywood produces a $300 million movie, there is such a massive overhead and architecture that goes into that, and it's incredibly cumbersome. When I try to make something, I try to make it very efficiently, and I try to test multiple ideas. Consequently a lot of those things don't work and fail. So, I have always looked at my failures as really growing experiences and part of a very positive experience. So sure, there's things that have not worked, but that's part of it.

One of the things that I would also advise, especially to young entrepreneurs, is that they need to treat their business very, very seriously from a legal and financial and accounting point of view. From the very earliest days have an attorney, have an accountant, be incorporated. Treat your business seriously. Too many people try and start their businesses, for example, without a tax ID or without a formal structure to it.

I think I see people like that fail. They either start and they get running and they don't have that legal and accounting grounding, and so they go off the rails either if they're successful or if they're not successful. We live in a world where too many mistakes can happen very quickly, so I would say attention to detail is key.

I'm trying to think of more concrete mistakes, but not a lot of things are coming to mind, because again, I do a lot of test and trial.

Stanley: Testing and tracking is the key.

Rob: Yes. The thing is it's easier and easier to do that. It doesn't take a lot, it just takes effort and knowledge and you can be online trying ideas for very little money.

Think about how much it would cost to start a traditional brick and mortar store. You have to rent the property and buy shelving and get your inventory up and market it and have a presence and staff it and then only find out if that little idea you had, works. That was the old way of doing it.

Now, you can go to something like Worldwide Brands, grab a bunch of products that fit a certain genre, put up an e-commerce store or an eBay store, use drop-shippers so you're not buying inventory, you take a little bit of time to invest in making it look good and you will see whether or not it works. You can tweak it and change it so quickly.

One of the most successful clients that we have, at one point he had 192 stores. 15 of them were profitable, but he had 192 that he was trying. He was always rotating in new things. This is the new world of selling.

Stanley: So the Internet has really made testing and tracking and direct response marketing a lot quicker and easier.

Rob: Yes. Absolutely. If you haven't read the book called The Long Tail by Chris Anderson... This is a wonderful book on really this whole concept of how to think about the very, very, very specific tastes that people have and selling to those very specific tastes.

LEARN, DO, LEARN, REDO

– *"Continually learn, and continually adjust your actions based on what you've got"*

Stanley: In your opinion, what are the three main ingredients to success as an Internet marketer?

Rob: Three main ingredients to success as an Internet marketer?

1. Learn as much as you can about the basics quickly
2. Do it. Try it. Get into it. Take action
3. Revise steps one and two

So, continually learn, and continually adjust your actions based on what you've got. This is a feedback society, right? Make sure you are getting feedback on what you're doing. Watch what happens, and follow the feedback that you're getting. So learn, do, and then learn and redo.

Stanley: Rob, I want to thank you for your time. Are there any final comments that you want to add or let people know about where they can get more information about you?

Rob: No. Please, thank you so much for your time. Please check out:

- Haxan.com
- SeventhMoon.com
- TheWorldwideBrands.com

We've got great customer service, seven days a week. You can call. Send us emails. We've got live people there, you can talk to and they will answer questions. But certainly engage us on every level and I wish everybody out there tremendous success. Again, I think I could not be happier or more excited about the world that we live in. Everywhere I look, I see so much opportunity because it's just getting better and better every day.

CHAPTER 12

ROSALIND GARDNER:
The Affiliate Marketing Queen

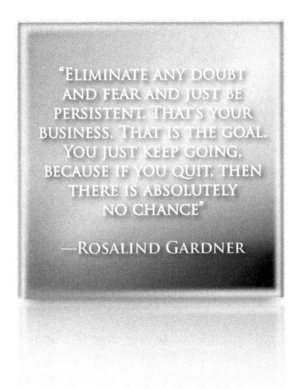

"ELIMINATE ANY DOUBT
AND FEAR AND JUST BE
PERSISTENT. THAT'S YOUR
BUSINESS. THAT IS THE GOAL.
YOU JUST KEEP GOING,
BECAUSE IF YOU QUIT, THEN
THERE IS ABSOLUTELY
NO CHANCE"

—ROSALIND GARDNER

ROSALIND GARDNER IS NOT ONLY AN EXTRAORDINARY WOMAN
*– she is the "Super Affiliate Queen" who works from home and makes a cool
six-figure income… selling other people's products!*

*Ros started out online back in 1998 with zero experience. She didn't know
how to build a website, had no idea what FTP, HTML or any of those terms*

meant – she certainly had never sold anything on the Internet. But her determination kept her going. Slowly but surely, her affiliate marketing business started to grow and went from $10.99 to over $500k+ in just a few short years!

Today, Ros teaches others how to become successful online through various courses, including her best-selling e-book *The Super Affiliate Handbook*. She is now also a frequent speaker at many Internet marketing seminars.

FROM AIR-TRAFFIC CONTROLLER TO INTERNET MARKETING

— *"I was looking for a way to leave my career because we were working some really crazy schedules"*

Stanley: Ros, can you tell us a bit about your background and how you got introduced to the Internet?

Rosalind: Actually, I've been online since the early '80s, back when we were doing bulletin boards and stuff like that. But I didn't get seriously involved until 1996. At the time I was an air-traffic controller and I was looking for a way to leave that career because we were working some really crazy schedules.

I built a little gardening site that managed to get an awful lot of traffic. As a matter of fact, it was a seed-exchange site. We were exchanging flower seeds because that's what I like to do is grow flower gardens. I basically saw the reach that you get with the web and decided to look at starting a business online, and the rest, as they say, is history.

Stanley: What did you do in your early days as an Internet marketer?

Rosalind: The very first thing I did, and that I'm still doing, is as an affiliate marketer, I was promoting Internet dating services.

Stanley: What was the dating service about?

Rosalind: At the time, I was single and I discovered that using a dating service

– like for single people looking to meet other people online – was a much better prospect than trying to meet somebody through a chat room or whatever. Atually, I saw a banner ad that said, "Webmasters make money."

It took me to the one-and-only dating service network affiliate program, which explained how you would make a portion of the sale as a commission if you managed to get people to sign up for this dating service. I thought, "Well, that's really cool. I can definitely promote that."

So I registered a domain, Sage-Hearts.com that's a weird name, I know. irst of all, I promoted just that dating service because that was really the only one I knew about, and then I started looking for other ones. Now, I think it's about 35 or 40 different dating services that I promote on that website.

Stanley: And was this back in 1998?

Rosalind: Yes, I started that site in '98. Actually, January 1, 1998, I decided that I was going to do that and I think I registered the domain a couple of days later. So it's been almost 10 years.

Stanley: What were some initial obstacles you've faced and how did you overcome them?

Rosalind: I had to learn everything from scratch. At the time, if there were courses about Internet marketing and how to build a website and all that, I didn't know about it. So when I was learning how to do HTML, I would do a "view source" on most of the websites that I saw, just in case I looked at the code and to learn about the code.

Everything that I did was by hand and learning it all from scratch. So it probably took me more time than it would have otherwise. Like nowadays, you can set up new blog in a minute. Right? Things are definitely faster nowadays and, of course, there's a whole lot more information about affiliate marketing.

Back in those days – I'm going to use the word regulated, not that it's overly regulated now – merchants could get away with a lot more, statistical reporting wasn't good, probably wasn't as secure. The industry has improved vastly in that amount of time.

WHAT IS AFFILIATE MARKETING?

— *"Affiliate marketing is probably best described as commission sales online"*

Stanley: For our readers out there, can you just briefly describe what affiliate marketing is and why is it so powerful?

Rosalind: Affiliate marketing is probably best described as commission sales online. So a merchant has a product that they want to promote and they're going to use affiliates, people like me and you and whoever to get them to promote their products. When the affiliate makes a sale, they earn either a commission or a percentage of the sale.

For example, with the dating services, when I was starting out, they were, generally speaking, 50 percent of the price of the dating service membership. So if the dating service membership sold for $25 per month, then I would have made $12.50 commission.

Sometimes you earn a referral fee, if you're just sending traffic and somebody has to put in their name and their email address. You can earn anywhere from $0.50 to $10 per referral for something like that.

Then there are times, such as for financial sites and services and credit cards, if you can get the visitor to your site to go to their site and fill in information or apply for a credit card and get approved, you can earn $40, $50, or $100 in some cases. So it's all about driving traffic and getting them to take action, either to buy a product or to fill in a form.

Stanley: After your success with the dating services, what did you do next?

Rosalind: I concentrated almost solely on that. Actually, that was all I did until 2003. In 2003 I published a book called, *The Super Affiliate Handbook: How I*

Made $436,797 in One Year Selling Other People's Stuff Online. I know it's a long title.

Since that time I have been helping webmasters through both my book and also through another website called NetProfitsToday.com, and basically just helping affiliates, primarily, but also anybody who wants to set up a blog or who wants to learn more about Internet marketing. So I've been working a lot on that end of things as well.

I also have a couple more affiliate websites going. One of them is a travel blog called Roamsters.com, which is another affiliate website. It's kind of actually like a journal. When I go on a trip, I blog about my trip and we have it monetized with some affiliate products, services and merchants products on which I'm earning commissions from that site as well.

THE SUPER AFFILIATE HANDBOOK

– *"That was really the intent of the book: To answer questions about affiliate marketing, because there really was no book that had that scope"*

Stanley: I just want to take you back a bit. You mentioned *The Super Affiliate Handbook*. Can you tell us a little bit about that? What you think was the main reason behind its success?

Rosalind: It was funny because I wrote that book in response to questions that I was getting from a profile that I did on the Internet Marketing Center's Secrets to Their Success website. I was interviewed and I talked about my business and how successful that was.

I guess not a lot of people had been talking about affiliate marketing back then – at least the successful affiliate marketers hadn't really been talking about their businesses, up until that point. So when my book came out – and of course, with the title about how I made $436,797 – it certainly captured people's interest.

From that point on, I started speaking at seminars such as Affiliate Summit. I actually had just got back from AdTECH in New York. The book was kind of immediately popular because I had Allan Gardyne of AssociatePrograms.com to help me promote. I sent him a copy and he actually refused to take my copy. He actually went out and bought a copy so that he could do a fair review.

I really appreciated that lesson in marketing, as a matter of fact, because if you want a non-biased review, you should really buy your own copy. So he gave it a really good review. He, of course, has a lot of affiliates and people who are interested in affiliate marketing on his list. So those people were interested in the book, and they got the book, and they began promoting the book.

Then I repeated that process a number of times, getting in touch with other affiliate marketers, other Internet marketers, whose audiences would have included people who were interested in affiliate marketing. So the book got a lot of exposure really quickly.

From there, I built the website for affiliate marketers shortly after that to answer more people's questions. And that was really the intent of the book: To answer questions about affiliate marketing because there really was no book that had that scope.

It still is probably the most thorough book on affiliate marketing. It gets updated and revised regularly, just to keep up with the times, because things seem to have changed greatly in these ten years. You can get a copy of that book over at TheSuperAffiliateBook.com.

Stanley: After your affiliate marketing book success, you launched a website called NetProfitsToday.com. What inspired you to do that?

Rosalind: The book, of course, couldn't answer all the questions. Nowadays, it actually shows you how to set up a blog; but, at that time, it wasn't about building a website. So a lot of these people who were interested in becoming affiliate marketers were also interesting in learning how to build a website.

So, I would get short questions through email and I thought, "Well, it would be better for me to put up a website and answer the questions there, so that more people could access that information, instead of just my answering every question one-by-one through email."

It has become quite a big website. I probably work on that website more than I work on anything else.

Stanley: After you created the NetProfitsToday site, what did you do next?

Rosalind: Other than the travel blog, that's about it. Those are my three main sites: The dating site, the NetProfitsToday.com site and the travel site. I don't have a staff. I have a virtual assistant, who helps me with customer service with the book, and a couple other products I sell online. Other than that, I don't have a big staff.

I've kind of limited myself to that and I recommend that for everybody. I think it's better to concentrate on one, two or three sites that you can build very large, with a lot of information, to draw a lot of traffic, than to build 50 or 100 or 200 or 1,000, in some cases, one-page sites, which require an awful lot of maintenance when things change and you have to go back and try to remember which site is which and logins and all of that stuff.

I think it's much easier just to have a few really good, valuable sites that are valuable for people who are interested in your particular topic.

TRAFFIC GENERATION TECHNIQUES
— *"The easiest way to get free traffic from search engines is to use blogs"*

Stanley: You have three websites. What were some of the ways you used to generate traffic and grow those websites?

Rosalind: Nowadays, the easiest way to get free traffic from search engines is to use blogs. Anik Singal and I did a blogging course called BlogClassroom. com, because we both have had such great success getting free search engine traffic to our blogs that we just thought it was so important that people start blogging, as opposed to putting up static HTML pages.

It's not my primary way of getting traffic. Very early, back when Yahoo! Search Marketing was GoTo.com, almost as soon as they came online, I started using them for pay-per-click marketing. In pay-per-click marketing, you bid on a search term. So, the term for my dating site was "dating service." There are others who are bidding on the term, so you want to get fairly good exposure and put yourself close to the top, so you have to bid above those people. That drives traffic to the dating site.

Then, as soon as they're at the dating site, what I want them to do is sign up for my newsletter so that I can keep getting in touch with them without having to spend any more money on pay-per-click advertising or any other type of ads. Of course, what I want them to do is come back, look at my blog and see what new products I'm writing about.

So basically, my three main ways of getting traffic are to drive it initially through pay-per-click and free search engine traffic from blogging, then continuing to contact them through email and my autoresponder series and through broadcast email messages.

THE SUPER AFFILIATE QUEEN!

— *"That's the number-one rule of selling: People buy from people they like and trust"*

Stanley: You are known as a super affiliate queen. What is the reason behind your affiliate marketing success? Can you share some your affiliate marketing strategies?

Rosalind: They're really basic. I don't look for a lot of tricks. I like to keep things fairly simple. Actually, my main motivation is: Keep it as simple as possible so you can take as much time off as possible."

A lot of people try to make things way too complicated and they get mucked down and mired down in the process with trying to tweak this and trying to tweak that, instead of just simply adding value by adding good content to their websites, in which people will be interested, and being real with people, rather than doing a glowing, good endorsement for a product with no negative aspects.

I always make sure that I'm really honest with people. If I don't like something about a product, I'll tell them. So, if I have two products, I compare them, I'll say, "Product A has all these features and benefits. I don't particularly like this but I like it better than Product B, which has all these features and benefits." And people really appreciate that more than anything. It's somebody online they feel they can trust.

That's how you make sales. That's the number-one rule of selling: People buy from people they like and trust. So that's what I've always tried to achieve: Just building up credibility among my readers. I like to create that relationship. I want to be somebody they can trust.

MISTAKES AND FAILURES

— *"The biggest thing is not to be scared of making mistakes because those are things that you learn from best"*

Stanley: What failures or mistakes have you made in the past, and what have you learned from them?

Rosalind: How much time do you have to spare? I think I've made every mistake there is. And that's actually one of the things that I like to talk about, especially on NetProfitsToday. You are bound to make mistakes because everything is changing so quickly. I think the biggest thing is not to be scared of making mistakes because those are things that you learn from best.

The very first big mistake that I made a long time ago was I bought software that would gather email addresses and then I kept those email addresses and I used another piece of software to contact all of those people via my Internet service provider, instead of using a viable or a good autoresponder service, like Aweber. I did it by my Internet service provider.

I was still working full-time at the time. I set this up to go with a couple of thousand addresses. It really wasn't that many. When I got home, I couldn't log on. I thought to myself, "What is going on here?" Well, they had shut me down and I wasn't going to be able to access the Internet through their service again.

They were the only provider in town, too, which was kind of a bad thing. I was living in a small town at that time. You are out of business if you don't have an Internet service or an Internet connection.

So I begged. I got on my knees and I said, "Please reinstate and I will never do that again." Of course, I never did. I am just so spooky. I had no idea that that was a bad thing to do. Oh yeah, I have made them all.

Stanley: What advice will you give to a beginner in Internet marketing?

Rosalind: First of all, be really interested in the topic that you are going to be blogging about or that you are going to start a website about. You will hear advice from other people who will say, "Oh, you don't have to know anything about a topic and you can just involve..."

I will step back here for a second. So many new Internet marketers start sites about Internet marketing when they know nothing about it. They have never made a buck online and yet they are trying to teach other people how to make money online, which is just completely bizarre because they have got no credibility and no one will ever trust them.

You really need to start a website about something that you are interested in. If you are a parent and you are writing about kids clothing or anything that you are passionate or very interested in is probably the best topic. It has to be something that you are going to be willing to talk about and write about for a fairly long period of time, if you want the site to go on for years and years, such as mine have done.

Then, just do it because there is only so much research and analyzing and this and that. Just get out there and start up that blog and learn along the way. Don't wait until everything is perfect because nothing is ever perfect.

I am constantly checking or changing my sites and working them around. That is just part of the process so that we can make changes and everything grows. So just get in there and be prepared to work.

I have come across a lot of people who think that it should all happen yesterday and that is not how it happens. You've got to spend time learning about the industry and learning how to make things work. There are a lot of pieces to be put together.

But it is not impossible because we all started from exactly the same spot and there are a lot of people who have become very successful. It is not beyond anybody's capability and it doesn't really require a whole lot of money to get started.

THE MINDSET AND BELIEF TO SUCCEED

— *"You've got to be determined, you've got to persevere, take action and you cannot quit"*

Stanley: In your opinion what mindset and belief should one have to succeed?

Rosalind: I probably already covered that. The mindset has to be a really positive attitude towards success. You've got to be determined, you've got to persevere, like you said, take action and you cannot quit.

You have to be realistic about whether or not your niche is going to work. Some of them just aren't viable and you should know that before you go into it. If you have done your homework and you have done the research on the niche, you know that there is a market and you can find your place within that market to build a successful website.

If, for whatever reason, you picked something that really isn't going to get that big, then you have to know when to quit. But more than anything, you really just have to, like I said, eliminate any doubt and fear and just be persistent. That's your business. That is the goal. You just keep going because if you quit, then there is absolutely no chance.

ENJOY YOURSELF

— *"We were put here to be happy and to be good to each other and be considerate and helpful"*

Stanley: What do you think is the importance of having fun?

Rosalind: I think that we were put here to be happy and to be good to each other and be considerate and helpful. I think I do a fairly good job of living my life that way. I make mistakes like everybody else.

But I think happiness is probably overrated. You are allowed to get mad and you are allowed to get upset and whatever else, but that doesn't mean that you are not happy and I don't think a lot of people understand that.

Stanley: Ros, I want to thank you for your time. Are there any final comments that you want to add or let people know about your main websites, where they can get more information about you?

Rosalind: If they are interested in my book, it is available at TheSuperAffiliateBook.com. Or actually, even if you go to RosalindGardner.com, you will find me there. Just Google my name, you will find me online and then you'll find me at a number of different places.

To the readers, enjoy yourself and just know that you can do this if you really, really want to and apply yourself.

CHAPTER 13

JEREMY SCHOEMAKER:
Founder of ShoeMoney Media Group

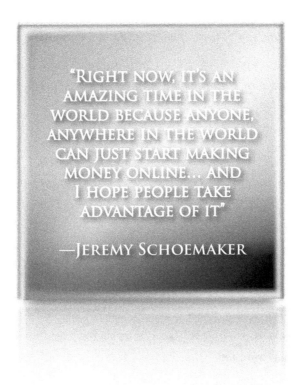

"RIGHT NOW, IT'S AN
AMAZING TIME IN THE
WORLD BECAUSE ANYONE,
ANYWHERE IN THE WORLD
CAN JUST START MAKING
MONEY ONLINE... AND
I HOPE PEOPLE TAKE
ADVANTAGE OF IT"

—JEREMY SCHOEMAKER

AFTER WORKING FOR THREE DIFFERENT INTERNET SERVICE
providers and numerous banks in the I.T. department, Jeremy Schoemaker found
himself on unemployment and without much income. Determined never to work
for "the man" again, he decided to make the break and ShoeMoney was born.

Now, Jeremy is recognized as one of the foremost authorities in the world when it comes to traffic monetization and affiliate marketing. He has taken on the world of Internet marketing with grit, determination and an uncanny knack for seeing marketing angles that most people do not.

To this day, Jeremy has:

- *Built a ringtone community site of over 60,000 paying members which generates over $2.7 million per year*
- *Cracked the AdSense code when he made over $132,994.97 in just one month*
- *Ranked in the Top 100 on Technorati.com for the blog ShoeMoney.com*
- *Launched a revolutionary eBay affiliate marketing service which was named "eBay Most Innovative Application – Buyers" (now bought out by MediaWhizz)*

His passionate desire to share his knowledge, coupled with his blog at Shoeoney.com, has helped thousands of people make money while pursuing their true passions in life.

FROM CUSTOMER SUPPORT TO SECURITY

– *"I was just always a kid who really liked technology and the Internet just kind of came into play with that"*

Stanley: Can I take you way back into your childhood? Tell us a bit about your background and where you came from.

Jeremy: Sure. I was born in Moline, Illinois, which is about 150 miles west of Chicago, as the crow flies. The area is very middle class and rundown. It's a big industrial labor area that really thrived with factories like International Harvester. It's the home of John Deere.

Since the late '80s, most of that labor was outsourced. And about the time I graduated high school, that area went through a massive depression. So, as far as jobs were, the market was flooded, and there were a lot of unemployment in the area. And I had a really tough time getting work. That would have been around the early '90s. I went away to college in 1994 to Western Illinois University.

I studied computer science, but I don't think I ever went to a class. I really liked political science classes and stuff like that. The computer classes really drove me crazy because they were talking about things that were 10 years old and stuff like that. It was really, really boring.

I was really an electronics nut, and I loved car audio and home audio. So I would build these crazy things inside my car, with speakers, and compete in competitions and stuff like that. I was just always a kid who really liked technology and stuff like that, and the Internet just kind of came into play with that.

I worked for three different startup Internet providers. In fact, I was selling washers and dryers at Sears, when a lady came in and offered me a job at an Internet provider because I was good with the Mac computers. I had no idea what the Internet was or what they were going to do. I was immediately just thrown into it and loved it from day one.

Stanley: What did you do in your early days online with the Internet providers?

Jeremy: I just did technical support. People would call in and I would walk them through setting up their point-to-point software from there. Mostly, I handled the Mac calls, but that was a very small portion of the customers, so I had to dive into everything – Windows, Linux and get to know those operating systems.

Then about three months later, I actually taught classes on using the Internet to mostly people that were middle-aged and older. It was a really big thing because the Internet was so new. We were teaching really simple things, like how to use email, what are bookmarks etc, but we would sell out every class.

What basically happened was, one night, the instructor called in sick, so I filled in teaching the class. They thought I did a really good job, so they had me do it from then on. It was good money because the instructor got half of the money for the class. I've always been good at communicating with people in-person, so I think that was a good fit for me back then.

For years, I continued teaching classes at night and worked during the day with the customer support, until I just needed more money. I had gone through three different providers in a couple years and I went back to school during that time as well.

When I came back, I basically wanted to work for more money. I got a job with a bank and was handling all their I.T. stuff. They really didn't have an I.T. staff. It was a small, regional bank in the Quad Cities in Illinois. There were around six or seven banks under my control. So basically, I just managed I.T. for all those banks and did everything from purchasing new computers, to servicing current computers, to going around networking, and all kinds of various stuff with that.

But that was a very interesting time because right then was when they had all this GBLA acts, which was basically like the Sarbanes-Oxley Act. It had all these compliance things and classifications of documents. So I had to go and get all this training. It was very high-level training on how to classify documents as protected, all these different classifications, and then write actual security policies. So, I found this little niche in the banking I.T. industry with security.

Then I switched from that job – I actually got fired. It's kind of an interesting way. I get all involved in my job and then I kind of lose interest after a while. But immediately when I was terminated from that job, I was scooped up by Wells Fargo at their headquarters because of my training and my pay rate doubled. So, it was like a win-win. Also, they moved me out of the depressed area that I was in.

I worked for them for years. Probably 90 percent of the security polices used within Wells Fargo were written by me. Basically, I trained employees and I did everything with security in computers. You named it. I was in the security division and was the lead for the UNIX systems and stuff like that.

I left there and moved to another bank in Nebraska and worked there for a couple of years. That's when I actually started doing business for myself on the side, and then finally made the transition fully to my own business.

BE YOUR OWN BOSS!
—   *"I just started making websites that I thought were cool services that people wanted to use"*

Stanley: Can you tell us about the transition? When was the breakthrough from your corporate life?

Jeremy: Like I said, I had worked for all these Internet providers previously, so I still had a computer set up at their place where they gave me free hosting on my own server. I had years and years of experience with UNIX and server-sides stuff, so I knew how to do a lot of programming. I wouldn't say I was a really good programmer, but I can hack and slash quite a bit.

I just started making websites that I thought were cool services that people wanted to use. My first one was a site called MacQuake.com. There's a popular game called Quake that was made by I.D. Software, but it was only for the Windows computers. Well, a bunch of hackers got together and they made a version for the Mac, which was a hack-off of the Linux version.

Of course, there was no support whatsoever from I.D. Software because it was a hacked version. So, I registered MacQuake.com, like the Macintosh Quake. I filed for an exception to their trademark policy and it was granted, so I could use the Quake trademark on my site. And it was great. We were doing good revenues in advertising and we were off and running.

That was kind of my first side business. Then I went from there and discovered that there was all this money in advertising and building quality sites. Shortly after that, I just started trying to make other sites. I got involved with a lot of mobile things, and tried to build mobile ringtones and wallpapers, and a big forum around that whole thing.

Eventually, I started to lose interest in my day job. Then finally, the last transition was just that the company I was working for got purchased. At that time, I actually went on unemployment for about two months while I was working on my own company, and I was able to finally draw a salary and establish that company.

Stanley: What were some initial obstacles that you faced and how did you overcome them?

Jeremy: Well, the biggest thing was a lack of social interaction because I was now working from home. I'm a very social person; I'm not a typical nerd that likes to just sit at home all day in the dark; I love hanging out with people. A lot of people who have ever met me at a conference will see that.

Also, managing time was difficult at first. It took me a while too. Because you're your own boss, therefore, if you want to sleep until noon, you can, as long as you're making money.

The financial burden is obviously a huge obstacle. At the time, when I started my company, my wife was still getting medical training. She was done with medical school, but had just started her anesthesia residency. So, she was hardly making any money, if any at all. My income was supporting the both of us. So, that was a huge burden to be put on.

That was about six or seven years ago. That was a huge transition and those were some huge obstacles.

THE DOT-COM CRASH!

– *"You can't put all your eggs in one basket. You need to diversify, and do a lot of due diligence with people that you're working with"*

Stanley: When the dot-com crash came at around 2000, you went through a lot of problem. Can you tell us about that and how you overcame it?

Jeremy: It basically ruined everything that I was doing at the time. That was when I had MacQuake.com and a couple of other sites. We were doing great online revenues. People weren't even asking for statistics at that time. They were just asking, "How much per month?" And you just shot them a price and they paid the bill.

That was awesome because I had no other money, other than just a few working here and there. But I was making more than everybody else – all my roommates combined. I thought I could do that for the rest of my life. Well, when the crash happened, it was really horrible. Companies not only wouldn't pay going forward, they wouldn't pay past bills. It really was a big, big problem.

I think some of the lessons learned from that were: You can't put all your eggs in one basket. You need to diversify and do a lot of due diligence with people that you're working with. Just little lessons like having advertisers pay ahead, things like that – big lessons learned from the crash.

THE BIRTH OF SHOEMONEY
— *"With the Internet, you never know what's going to happen"*

Jeremy: We were doing good revenues, or at least what I thought at the time was good. It was definitely more than I was making at my previous day jobs. My wife was going to be a physician. The plan was basically that I was going to be the stay-at-home dad and work from home, and she was going to make the good money.

We basically created a company to make the personal and the business stuff separate, because I needed to protect her assets. With the Internet, you never know what's going to happen. We've been sued a couple of times; we've sued people. There are a lot of crazy things that can happen on the Internet. So that was definitely a big thing: Incorporating ShoeMoney Media, so that it separated personal and business.

Stanley: What really inspired you to come up with the name ShoeMoney?

Jeremy: Actually, it's kind of funny how ShoeMoney came about. The area I'm from is a very urban area and I always grew up listening to rap music and stuff like that. I was probably pretty influenced by it.

I was working one day at a pizza place, cutting pizzas, when I was 15 years old. After they came out of the oven, they would put them on this thing and I would cut them up. I was pretty efficient at it. So, they used to always put me on the cut table.

One Christmas, a guy who worked there we had like a secret Santa swap his name was Joe Ackerman. Basically, he gave me the nickname "ShoeMoney" and he gave me a T-shirt for Christmas that said, "ShoeMoney on the Cut" (Like ShoeMoney on the cut table). It was kind of a funny thing.

Source: Shoemoney.com

I had already been drawing the ShoeMoney logo since I was 12 years old. I thought it was cool. It looked like Superman but it was money. My original site was actually ShoeMoneyMedia.com and my actual blog, when I first started, was GoogleNinja.com.

A friend of mine said, "You shouldn't use Google because they'll sue you." And I said, "OK." What I did was I backordered ShoeMoney.com. One day, the person who had the domain name let it expire. I got a notice from GoDaddy saying that I was the new owner and I switched over from GoogleNinja.com to ShoeMoney.com. And that would have been a couple of years ago.

THE GOOGLE CHECK:
$132,994.97 IN ONE MONTH FROM ADSENSE

— *"We were constantly seeing $3 to $5 per click throughout that month. That was a pretty crazy month"*

Stanley: On your blog, there's a picture of you holding the famous $132,995 Google check. Can you tell us a bit about the story behind that?

Jeremy: Sure. That was on a site called NextPimp.com, which is a mobile community site. The most we had ever brought in from AdSense was about $60,000 to $70,000 a month. The traffic was purely organic using search engine optimization. There was no pay-per-click advertising. In fact, I didn't even know what pay-per-click was back then.

Basically, it was a Nextel-geared site. At that time, Sprint had just merged with Nextel, and the cost-per-click for all Nextel terms just went through the roof. I don't know if they were just dumping the budget or what happened, but we were constantly seeing $3 to $5 per click throughout that month. That was a pretty crazy month.

That was also the last time we ran AdSense because that was when all these companies realized the value of ringtones. That was really when they started, and so people were spending money like crazy to acquire users in their services. After that month, we signed a direct deal with Sprint and other carriers to only show their banners exclusively.

BLOGGING: CRACKING THE TOP 100 ON TECHNORATI

— *"Direct ad sales for blog is the number-one best way to make money"*

Stanley: Your blog ShoeMoney.com is ranked in the top 100 on Technorati. How did you first get into blogging?

Jeremy: In 2005, I went to my first conference, to San Jose SES and, while I was there, this guy showed me his blog. Back then, I thought blogs were the stupidest thing in the world. I was like, "So, you put your thoughts on this?" And he was like, "Yeah." And I'm like, "And people care about what you write?" And he was like, "Yeah." And that just didn't make sense to me.

But I did want to put up all my photos from things that I've done, like conferences I had attended and things like that. Then I thought, "Well, maybe there is a little value in a blog because my mom and other family members are always asking me what I'm doing. And I hate explaining it to all of them because it's hard and stuff like that. Well, I'll just start this blog for me, and it'll be a place where I can vent and just talk about my theories on things from my experience."

So, that's how it started. I just put it up. My first post I ever made was about how I met Paris Hilton in Las Vegas nothing to do with making money online. You know what I mean? A lot of the times, I don't post about making money online and stuff like that, but just more my personal blog kind of thing. So, that's how it started, anyway.

Stanley: What do you think was the biggest reason behind the success of your blog ShoeMoney.com?

Jeremy: I think the blog is successful. It's difficult how you measure success. It depends if it's because of advertising or just because of its popularity. I think the blog is successful because, for one, it's a good story.

I basically chronicle how, if you look at my life before, I was 420 pounds plus, I smoked 10 packs of cigarettes a day and I was hundreds of thousands of dollars in debt. And I went from that. I lost weight and I'm now a very fit person and very health-conscious. We make great money. You know what I mean? I think it's just kind of the dream. I don't have a college degree – I barely graduated high school – I was probably voted "most likely to never amount to anything" if there was a poll on that from my high school.

It's just everybody can relate to it, whether you've gone through that yourself or you're looking to improve yourself. I think that I have a pretty interesting story and I've worked really hard to get where I'm at. People like success stories. So I think that's one of them.

The other thing is, I started writing this blog back when I wasn't making very much at all. I was just selling computers on eBay. There are people that have been reading the blog since the early days, so a lot of them actually grew with me over the years. We went not only from just discovering how to make money online, but to owning our own companies and competing with the biggest companies and then selling those companies.

There are a lot of people that write about making money online and I think one of the differences in that space, with my blog and a lot of others, is we actually not only do it, but we're very transparent about exactly what we do well, I am anyway, probably too much to the point. During the time I've had my blog, we went from just me as an employee to, now, we have five employees and two offices throughout the U.S.

Stanley: What are some of your ways to generate traffic to your blog?

Jeremy: I would say I don't intend to but that's probably a cheap way out. As far as generating traffic, I used to try to get on Digg every day. For a month, I was obsessed with Digg and I think we got on the homepage maybe 10 days out of the whole month. It was pretty crazy. But then you measure the quality of that traffic: It's junk; it totally rapes your server; it ruins it for the people that are loyal.

Another key way for anyone who's looking to write an educational kind of blog is that you have to find different ways to approach old subjects, because the information is always been out there. You just have to find a way to present it to people in a way that they've never heard it, or in a way they can now comprehend and understand it. It could be from a different angle or something like that.

I'm trying to directly answer the question of how I generate traffic, but I really don't set out to like, "Oh! This will be awesome! This will generate a lot of traffic!" because the blog is a very small portion of our company and our company's income. I really have to limit my time and spending. So generating traffic to the blog is not a huge priority.

Stanley: What are some of your ways to monetize that traffic apart from Ad-Sense?

Jeremy: Well, it depends on what we are talking about. For a blog, like I said, the blog is not my main thing, but I've definitely learned how to make money on it.

For a blog that gets attraction, the best way by far is direct sales. Everybody who has AdSense or anything should also have a page where people can buy directly from you for permanent placement, because usually you can sell it for more money and, if you get any readership at all, usually companies will want to be displayed there. So, direct ad sales for blog is probably the number-one best way to make money.

NEXTPIMP.COM

— *"The key to having a successful forum is: You've got to give"*

Stanley: What about for some of your other sites like NextPimp.com?

Jeremy: Sure. For NextPimp.com, the best way that we have made money on that site was through subscription revenue. We actually charge for forum subscriptions and we have about 60,000 paying subscribers.

People freaked out on the AdSense check and thought that was an amazing thing. And it is. I can definitely see why and it was to me at the time. It was huge. Now we have 60,000 paying members, which accounts for about $2.7 million a year in revenue, which is purely auto-reoccurring.

For community sites, subscription is by far the smartest form of making money. You really have to do your research on price points and times (how long is a subscription going to go for until it is renewed). We changed our price points and plans on NextPimp.com several times before we finally found the sweet spot.

Stanley: What do you think is the biggest key to the success of a community site?

Jeremy: You have to have a good niche or something else around. You can't just put up a forum. For instance, if you look at the Digital Point forums, which are the most trafficked webmaster forums out there, that didn't start out as a forum. That website provided all kinds of great tools. That's how I started using it.

They have a keyword tracker and all these SEO tools that you can use. So, I started just by using some of their tools. Then you get sucked into the forums because they show recent posts and stuff like that. One of those will eventually spark your interest and you'll sign up and give your two cents. That's how I started on Digital Point and that's what drew me in.

So, in the case of NextPimp.com, we had all the content of ring tones and wallpapers and mobile content and all this stuff. I threw up a forum with the same concept and through recent threads with the content. It kind of gets people sucked into the forum. People either need help with the content or they can't get it to their phone or they want to sell their phone or whatever. You give them an outlet for that.

Now, with our most recent project, Fighters.com, we are going to build a huge mixed martial arts site; we are going to build a forum and a community around great content.

So, the key to having a successful forum is: You've got to give. You've got to have an edge or a niche which draws people other than just a place where people can chat because they can get that anywhere. You have to definitely have some sort of niche, focused, good content, and all that stuff around the forum.

AUCTIONADS.COM
— *"It was one of the most successful launches of an advertising company ever"*

Stanley: You started a site called AuctionAds.com, which eventually got bought out. Can you tell us a bit about that?

Jeremy: Sure. Like we talked about previously, I did good AdSense revenues and realized the value of it. This is how AuctionAds got started:

You take AdSense. It works awesome. When you look at it, you think, "Why does it work so well?" Well, the text format and everything looks great. So, one day, I said to Dave, who is my programmer, "You know, let's make our own AdSense system but let's do affiliate offers instead because pretty much everybody who was advertising on our sites was all going to affiliate offers."

"OK, these guys are making money advertising on our site. We think we are getting paid good money, but actually they are the ones making really good money. Let's just cut out them, cut out Google and make our own thing." And we did. We called it ShoeMoney Ads.

That was March of 2005. We actually created a company and we allowed people to use it themselves. So they could upload any affiliate code and write their own text. It was basically AdWords and AdSense for your own website. We really limited the amount of people that could use it. I think it was only open to about 250 people.

Shortly after that, November of 2005, at the WebmasterWorld PubCon Conference, there were some representatives from eBay there. They said to us, "We really like your ShoeMoney Ads platform. If you want to make one targeted more towards eBay – the people that are using it for eBay now are doing really well with it – we would work with you with that." And we think it would work.

At the time, they were not allowing anyone really to do what they were going to allow us to do. I figure it was only because we had had a record of success with ShoeMoney Ads.

But there were a couple of problems. One, we are not good at customer support or service. We are kind of programmers and people like that. As social as I am, we just suck at that. So, that was a problem. The other one was, we had never done an advertisement system. We didn't know how to send out mass payments or anything like that.

We could handle the programming side and the marketing side because I have Dave to do programming and myself to do marketing. But we didn't know how to handle the financial aspects of it or the customer support.

So, I talked to a friend of mine, Patrick Gavin of TextLink Ads, whose company was bought by MediaWhiz, and said to him, "We have this idea. I think it's going to be awesome." So he was onboard with it. Then the company that had bought his company, MediaWhiz, entered into a partnership with us and started the company called AuctionAds, which basically was somewhat like AdSense but with eBay. For those that haven't seen it, it shows how much time there's left on auctions, what the current price is and stuff like that.

They owned a minority stake in it. We kicked them off. Within four months, we had 25,000 users doing revenues of millions per month. By July, only four months after we had launched it, MediaWhiz, who owned the minority, bought out my shares in the company. So I only owned it for four months.

But I think it was one of the most successful launches of an advertising company ever. And I think the reason was because the Internet is driven by the world economy. There are all these advertising platforms that only cater to the U.S. for the most part. Even though AuctionAds was single to just things on eBay, because eBay was located in 12 countries and we were able to geo-target that through our programming resources, we now had an advertising solution that had a huge amount of inventory. It was located in 12 countries that you could monetize it with.

As far as being a global option, it really had no competition, because there was really nothing else that offered that in a one-solution deal. Plus, we also saw the problems in the pay-out structure. We paid people net zero terms, which nobody has ever done that. On the first of the month, we would pay people for the previous month's things. I think a lot of users really loved that. Then we incentivized some of the users.

I think a lot of our techniques are now being copied by new start-up advertising companies. We had a lot of calls from companies and stuff like that. But it was a really interesting company to start. I'm glad, obviously, that it was really successful.

THE FUTURE OF SHOEMONEY

— *"We created a company called ShoeMoney Capital, which basically fund people that are trying to start up new ideas through assets, whether it's money, marketing or programming experience"*

Stanley: What are some of your future plans to taking your company to the next level?

Jeremy: With the sale of AuctionAds and our other companies, we have quite a bit of capital and a lot of experience. I think I'm one of the best marketers online and I think I also have one of the best programmers for e-commerce, Dave Dellanave.

Now, between us, we have money, programming and marketing. Those are basically what every start-up company needs. So we created a company called ShoeMoney Capital, which basically can fund people that are trying to start up new ideas through assets, whether it's money, marketing experience or programming experience.

We've done that with a few companies. We incorporated ShoeMoney Capital. We haven't even gotten a website up yet and I don't know if we will. Right now, we're working with Liquor.com and other companies that we're looking at taking a stake in and offering our resources there. I think that's probably the future of ShoeMoney, is taking our experience and being a part of some of these sites.

I went to a conference called the Tech Crunch 40, where basically all these companies demoed their products. There were some really awesome, amazing ideas. The problem is a lot of them didn't know how to make money or they were having programming issues or they were broke. They were all a week away from being bankrupt for the most part.

I retained a couple of their info and maintained contact with them and will probably be investing in them. I think that's a really big thing because there are all these great ideas and great sites that just don't have the marketing and financial resources or the programming experience to really make it work.

I think that we can offer that and take a stake. It's not venture capital. It's probably closer to what is referred as angel funding. I think that's probably our future.

SUCCESS: THE SHOEMONEY WAY

– *"One of the biggest keys to being a successful marketer is understanding the psychology of the people that you're trying to market to"*

Stanley: What do you think are the three main ingredients to success as an Internet marketer?

Jeremy: I think one of the biggest things is people close themselves off and think they know everything. I think one of the biggest reasons people become successful is always listening and watching everything. Don't be so judgmental.

A lot of times, you'll hear people and they'll say, "Oh, I read this e-book and this guy is an idiot." And things like that. I'm always a little disturbed by that because I read pretty much every e-book and I always get something out of it. Usually, it has nothing to do with what the person is saying but they'll trigger something in me.

I think passion is another keyword, too. If you're not passionate about what you're doing – basically, you wouldn't be doing it for a hobby – then, I think you won't be successful. For me, marketing is a hobby. I love it. I love selling. I love marketing. And I love psychology.

So really, to answer your question, I think one of the biggest keys to being a successful marketer is understanding the psychology of the people that you're trying to market to. If you can do that, then everything else is very, very easy.

A WEEK IN THE LIFE

– *"I like to keep in touch and surround myself with successful people"*

Stanley: Can you walk us through a typical day in your life?

Jeremy: Well, it would probably be easier to take you through a quick week. Every day, the plan is to get up at 7am, but my daughter, who's 20 months old, will get up anywhere from 6:30 to 7:30. So I get up with her, spend about an hour with her and then our nanny arrives. Then I go to work. I've got an office downtown that I work at.

Usually, the first thing I do is check the revenue from the previous day to make sure everything is on track and make sure there are no weird anomalies going on. Then from there, I touch base with Dave, who's now pretty much my partner in the company, to see how he's doing, what he's doing, or if he needs anything from me, or if I haven't delivered anything I said I would, pretty much anything what's going on.

Ty, who works for me full-time, has an office here as well. I check in with him to see how things are going. He's managing the Elite Retreat, so he's pretty busy with that right now.

I usually take a lunch at about 11am to 1pm. I usually have a lot of meetings over lunch here locally, with some local friends that are also in business, as well. I like to keep in touch and surround myself with those successful people. Then, after lunch, usually it's just whatever we're working on. I'll touch back in with Dave and whatever needs being done.

I'll make calls. A lot of time is spent on the phone during the day, just kind of connecting things so that other people in my company can do their job better. It's just a lot of oversight. I do most of the marketing firsthand, but Dave handles all the programming and stuff. Then I have Ty, who's doing a lot of the footwork for a lot of our projects now.

Monday, Wednesday and Friday, I knock off around 4:30 and come home and spend time with my kids. Then I go to the gym from 5:30 to 7pm. Then I come home and spend two hours with my wife. Then when she goes to sleep, which is really early, about 8pm to 9pm, I'll go back to work usually until about 1am. Sometimes it goes later, sometimes earlier.

That's kind of my fun time, working time online, where I'll read blogs or read forums, and just kind of my relax time. I'll hack and slash on some code and build some silly little thing.

Then on Tuesdays, I do a radio show. So on Tuesday, my schedule is really crazy because I work, then I work out and then do my radio show. Then there's an Elite Retreat mastermind call, which was actually formed by the previous attendees of the Elite Retreat, and they do a once-a-week call where they all kind of touch in and talk about what they're working on and they all kind of make assignments for each other. It's really, really good, and it's been something that I've adapted and started participating in.

That's pretty much my week. Friday and Saturday nights, especially Sundays, I try to spend as much time as possible with my family. It's still hard, but with things like smart phones and stuff like that, you can do a lot being mobile and kind of relaxed. So that's pretty much my life.

JUST START DOING

— *"You don't have to quit your day job. I think that's actually a huge mistake by most people. You can do it in line, just do it when you have time and see how it works. Everything starts off very small"*

Stanley: Jeremy, I want to thank you for your time. Got any final comments you want to add, or let people know about your main website, where they can get more information about you?

Jeremy: Sure. I think the future right now, I encourage anyone who is looking at creating extra income, if you're really passionate about a subject, just start writing about it. You don't have to quit your day job. I think that's actually a huge mistake by most people. You can do it in line, just do it when you have time and see how it works. Everything starts off very small.

Also, right now, I think it's an amazing time, because anyone, anywhere in the world, can just start making money online, or at least try and come up with some good techniques and stuff like that. It's just an amazing time in the world and I hope people take advantage of it because I hope there's not a lot of people, which I'm sure there will, 10, 15 years ago, saying, "I had this great idea back then and I didn't do it because I was lazy."

So, in closing, I'd just like to encourage everybody to do that. My blog is at ShoeMoney.com and that's pretty much it. Thanks for having me, Stanley.

CHAPTER 14

ANDREW FOX:
Internet Super Affiliate

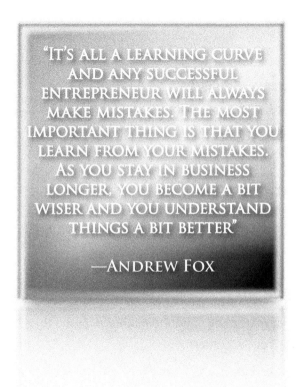

"IT'S ALL A LEARNING CURVE
AND ANY SUCCESSFUL
ENTREPRENEUR WILL ALWAYS
MAKE MISTAKES. THE MOST
IMPORTANT THING IS THAT YOU
LEARN FROM YOUR MISTAKES.
AS YOU STAY IN BUSINESS
LONGER, YOU BECOME A BIT
WISER AND YOU UNDERSTAND
THINGS A BIT BETTER"

—ANDREW FOX

EIGHT YEARS AGO, HE WAS WASHING CARS FOR $5 PER HOUR.

Eight years later, he lives the Internet lifestyle.

At just 26 years old, Andrew Fox has managed to buy a luxurious beach front home, travel first-class around the world, and buy not one, but two incredible Ferraris.

But here's the crazy thing – he's winning affiliate contests and pulling in $70,697, $29,013 and $90,388 commission profit pay days…on a regular basis while he's away from the computer and traveling around the world!

And it wasn't so long ago when Andrew took a $200 resell rights product and turned it into a $25,000 payday.

How did he do this? How was he able to go from car washer to living the rock star lifestyle?

I had to find out.

GETTING STARTED ONLINE

— *"If you can make $100, you can make $1,000, you can make $1,000,000. It's just finding that formula that works and scaling it up and replicating it"*

Stanley: Tell us a bit about your background and how you got started online with Internet marketing.

Andrew: Well, I actually began in 1999, which was about eight years ago. I used to wash cars for $5 per hour and then I was working in an exhibition Blockbuster store where they rent DVDs and videos.

I got started when I was working originally with a business partner, and we just started finding ways of marketing on the Internet. We were typing in key-words like "Internet marketing" and the main guy at the time was Corey Rudl of The Internet Marketing Center.

I got really hooked on his stuff. It was eight years ago around Christmas when I ordered these London DVDs from Corey Rudl that explain how an Internet business works. I was sitting Christmas Day and I was watching these videos and I was getting really excited about the vast potential on the Internet. That's how I got started there.

Our first website was something called GetMarketTips.com, which was a website where people would pay for a membership to gain access to these tools that we'd created and would get traffic to your website. It sold pretty well. We were pulling at least $20 to $40 per day to start off with.

The first big hit that we had in April 2000 was where we released a website called UltimateMailer.com. Using all the marketing experience we had learned from people like Corey Rudl and Yanik Silver as well – he was a good mentor to me – we put everything together and when we launched the website back then, we made around $15,000 the first month, which was incredible, even after eight years of this – that was an awesome amount.

Stanley: What did you do in your early days? What obstacles did you face and how did you overcome them?

Andrew: It's quite interesting because eight years ago it was very different to what it is now. People now get so bored with information and offers. Every single day, there are so many spams in their email inbox and there are so many marketers who are trying to get you to buy their products. But, eight years ago, it was maybe 2 percent of that. There was information there, but it was nowhere near as much.

There was Yanik Silver, who had a course, and Corey Rudl, and a few other people like Jonathan Mizel and Marlon Sanders. They were the people who got started very early on. It's hard to get started. But, as soon as you can start making some money and you know what you're doing right, it's just a matter of scale.

My friend, John Reese, he always talks about that. If you can make $100, you can make $1,000, you can make $1,000,000. It's just finding that formula that works and scaling it up and replicating it.

People come online and they want to make money but they need to find their niche because even in Internet marketing. Do you want to learn how to optimize websites for search engines and make AdSense income? Do you want to become a consultant by being an expert in your field? Do you want to become a copywriter? Do you want to sell information products? Do you want to sell products like pay-per-click marketing? You need to find out what you're naturally better at and stick with it.

Stanley: Yes. Afterwards, what did you do next?

Andrew: After UltimateMailer.com, that was 2000, we worked on that website for a while. We made little improvements such as trying to get more traffic to the website. We tried some pay-per-click advertising. I changed the sales letter and tried to up the conversion rate. I also started selling different memberships at different prices.

There's just a lot of testing and stuff. We released a series of products. I've done a lot of things from having my own information products to buying resale rights to products and making a small fortune with them. Over that eight years, I've done a lot of things.

HOW TO TAKE A $200 RESALE RIGHTS PRODUCT AND GENERATE $25,000

— *"More and more joint venture partners were seeing this; everybody wanted to get on board promoting this AdSense Profit Guide"*

Stanley: How did you first get introduced to ClickBank?

Andrew: We actually used ClickBank back in 2000 for UltimateMailer.com. ClickBank has grown a lot larger now, but what I absolutely love about Click-Bank is a few things.

First of all, they have a built-in affiliate program where you can harness the power of their affiliate force. There are a lot of people out there who explore the ClickBank marketplace, looking to promote products with an affiliate. Click-Bank takes care of your affiliates. They handle your refunds. They look after all the bookkeeping side. On a smaller scale that might not sound like a lot, but when you start to build things up, it's a lot of paperwork and admin.

That's sort of how our friendship started. I didn't work with them as much then. For a few years I was trying other things. But I find ClickBank to be so reliable in terms of paying you like clockwork every two weeks with a check. They handle affiliate payments and they are easy to deal with. So that's why I work with them and why I continue to work with them. They are a great place.

Stanley: Just then, you mentioned about resale rights products. You previously took a $200 resale rights product and generated almost $25,000. Tell us a bit about the story behind that.

Andrew: That was pretty interesting, Stanley. I look at those numbers and it blew me out of the water. It's just keeping your eyes open and your ear to the ground. What I mean by that is you've got to see what the market wants at the time. At the time, Google AdSense was absolutely chaotic. You could set up a website about Google AdSense and just put on a picture of something and people would buy it.

I got an email from a guy called Ryan Deiss. Ryan Deiss is a very good and competent friend and he said that it was $200 for resale rights to the product and you could sell it for $27 each. I reckoned I could sell quite well. So what I did was, I got the product. I put it up in ClickBank. The good thing about this is, you don't have to own the product to sell it in ClickBank; you can just own an exclusive resale rights license to the product.

So I got the product up in ClickBank. I created a page for affiliates with a few banner ads, email ad copy. Then I promoted it to my own lists that I had, and I started contacting joint venture partners, going, "Hey, I've got this product that's a reselling item, but it sells and converts very well. Do you want to promote it?"

And because it sold very well, and more and more joint venture partners were seeing this, everybody wanted to get on board promoting this AdSense Profit Guide. By the time everything was finished, I'd made about $25,000 in sales. So it was pretty incredible how it just evolved.

THE POWER OF MEMBERSHIP SITES

— *"Membership sites allow you to work more freely on other projects. It's also a good idea to build trust and member loyalty"*

Stanley: Later on, you launched a membership site called CB Affiliate Formula, at TheCBFormula.com. What is the membership site about? How were you able to create a huge buzz?

Andrew: Well, I've been asked for years to do personal coaching. Usually, because I'm always busy working on a project, I didn't have the time to do that. The main thing is getting the right infrastructure. If you have a membership website, again, managing your members and getting fresh content and stuff. It is a task that you've always got to work at.

So from ClickBank, actually I'd say recurring billing fit into my model well, because I sell a lot of products through ClickBank. The demand was growing over time. I had reselling products like HowtoResell.com, which was an e-book, like a step-by-step blueprint of selling in Internet Business. And another product called DominatingCB.com, which was a nine-video tutorial showing people how to begin selling products through ClickBank.

So there was a great demand for coaching clubs. That's why I decided to really work at it and put something together and create the CB Affiliate Formula.

Stanley: Speaking of membership sites, what is the power of membership sites and recurring income?

Andrew: Everything in life, when you have a house or you have a car, you always have monthly bills, and you always want to have money coming in to pay those bills. Recurring income is a great way to free you up more, because you know you have a certain amount of income per month, regardless of whatever your other projects are. It means that you can relax.

It also allows you to work more freely on other projects. It's a good idea to build trust and loyalty because it's nice to interact with people and spend time answering their questions and helping them grow their businesses.

I try to spend a lot of time and I have the offer open: Anybody can send me a private message in the forum inside of the membership site, and I always get back to them as soon as I can and help them grow their business. So it's good to build member loyalty.

It's good for residual income. It offers at least an opportunity where they can promote once and get paid for the life of the member, as long as they stay on. Affiliates like that as well. So it really is a win-win situation all around.

BECOMING A SUPER AFFILIATE

— *"What I do is, when I want to learn how to do something, I study someone who is already successful"*

Stanley: In CB Affiliate Formula, you teach people how to do affiliate marketing and things like that. What's the biggest reason behind your success as a super affiliate?

Andrew: Well, it's pretty interesting. What I do is, when I want to learn how to do something, I study someone who is already successful. If I want to become a successful property investor, I look at the people who are successful and then I contact them and ask them, and I definitely grill their brains until there is no more.

I study people who are making big affiliate paydays, like John Reese, Chris McNeeney and Ewen Chia. What I noticed is that a lot of marketers out there really are losing. When they come into the affiliate program, they just wait until the day the product releases, and then they just send the same ad copy that the other marketers are sending. That diminishes your conversion rate, because a reader is going to be on several other people's lists, so they're just going to see the same ad from 10 pitches. That means you're doing it the same as everybody else.

You've got to differentiate from the crowd. I like to have my own bonuses. I like to give mini-reviews of the product. I like to inject my own personality. I like to tell people weeks in advance. I always test the product out and make sure it's a completely high-quality product and a fit for my list. I explain the benefits. I talk to them about why they should get it. I explain the value in the product. I never just get generic ad copy and copy-paste-send – it's just criminal to do that.

Stanley: Also, you should never promote junk products to your list.

Andrew: Oh, yeah. You've got to realize that if you promote rubbish to your list, they're going to know that. If you promote the product as an affiliate, and they use that, and even if they refund that product, it doesn't matter, because as long as you explain why they should buy it and you've delivered an honest opinion and that you were looking out for them, they will buy from you again. You've always got to put the customer first. Customer first, money later, that's the way you should do business.

THE POWER OF FOCUS WITH A TO-DO LIST

— *"You've got to have a very methodical and focused mindset. It's a critical part of being successful and maintaining success"*

Stanley: Can you describe a typical day in your life?

Andrew: It varies quite a lot. Some weeks, I work every day. I get up and usually go and pick up one of my employees and we come round and sort of run through maybe 10 minutes, sort of tasks for the day. I sit down, go through my email first, delete all the junk and keep the important stuff. To keep me focused, I always write out lists of things I should get to during the day and get completed.

You need to divide your time up. For example, "I need to spend a certain amount of time writing the emails to my list, or I need to spend a certain amount of time per day going on my own membership website, to market and improve what kind of content I need to have etc."

Other days – I have a beautiful yacht – I just go down to Dublin, Ireland (Andrew is from Ireland) and I have wireless Internet access. I just get down there and relax and almost let the sea inspire me and see what I want to create next. So it's great the way you can mix in your business with your own lifestyle.

Stanley: You talked about creating a to-do list. What is the power of creating a to-do list?

Andrew: It's absolutely critical. Anybody reading, if you come home from work and you can spend one or two hours per night, you should write a list. For example, "Spend 30 minutes reading this e-book and make notes." Or, "Contact one joint venture partner per day." Or, "Try and learn how to do this."

People get distracted so easily. Rick Schefren was releasing a new report called The Attention Age. The Internet has become so noisy and there are so many offers and so many thing being slammed in your face, people just become oblivious to it. So, as a person, you need to sit down and you need to focus and take it one step at a time.

If you're a beginner, it can be to service your email list, or learning how to sell to your subscribers, or learning how to affiliate market. You need to set up a game plan and find out what's working for you and then start filling it up. Just become a focused, methodical person.

When your business gets bigger, people sometimes see you and they see those nice cars or boat or something, and they think, "Oh, that guy's doing really well. It's a great lifestyle." And yes, it is, but there's a lot of work behind it. You've always got to keep in touch, like keeping your forums and your contacts and keeping your business affairs in order. You're always looking and planning for taxes and stuff. That's another side of business as you grow bigger that you've got to look out for.

Stanley: In your opinion, what mindset and beliefs should one have to succeed in Internet marketing?

Andrew: A lot of people tell me – and I can understand why I do get the problems – there's a lot of crap out there. The other problem is that there's also a lot of good stuff. But if you're given 12 different courses, you can't just read them all at once and apply it. As I say, you need to have a very focused mindset and positive thinking.

You've got to think of it as, when you see somebody making money from AdSense or something, it is a phase and it kind of goes past at some stage. So you've got to set yourself up. Build your own brand name; build your own subscriber list – talk to them, because that's like a real asset. If something crash, then you've still got your customer list and you've got your brand name and loyalty.

So it's very important to have a focused mindset and say, "Hey, look, I want to build a business. I want to establish myself as an authority on what I'm doing. I want to build my email list this much per day. I want to know how to convert subscribers into buyers." Become focused. It's a critical part of being successful and maintaining success.

POSITIVE ATTITUDE AND MOTIVATION
– *"Visualization is a critical part of keeping a mental positive attitude"*

Stanley: You mentioned about positive attitude. How can one stay and maintain a positive attitude?

Andrew: Sometimes when you're working, anybody in the world can get distracted or get bored or unmotivated. What I like to do is I have a picture of a car or some boat on the wall, something I want to achieve, that's what my end goal is. I actually spend a lot of time looking at it. I'm a Ferrari enthusiast, so sometimes I spend the time looking around at different Ferraris. I search the Internet for 15 minutes, just to motivate my mind and show me what I can achieve.

Some people will want things like Ferraris and boats and stuff like that, or they want to move into their dream home. Other people just want to make enough money to pay a few extra bills or take their family on a holiday. So if that's you and you want to take your family on a holiday, go and locate your dream vacation and put it up on your wall, because visualization is a critical part of keeping a positive mental attitude.

Stanley: So you always take some time to try to visualize your future and what you want your future to be like.

Andrew: It's very true. It's the power of manifestation: Learning to visualize what you want and going after it. You'll never get there in a straight line. There's always going to be complication along the way. Some products might sell really well; some products might not sell as well for you. But as long as you maintain your end goal then you can get there.

OVERCOMING SUCCESS

— *"Happiness is not related to the amount of money. It's just whatever your personal goal is"*

Stanley: What was the lowest point in your life, and how did you overcome it? Can you talk a bit about that?

Andrew: The lowest point in my life? It's quite interesting. I achieved success and the low point at almost the same time. When I was working towards buying my dream home – which I achieved – I had one time when I stopped sleeping. I was working non-stop; I was working 18-hour days at the time. I was very devoted and focused.

When I achieved my dream house, I could hardly relax because I had stressed my body out so much from working. I was finding it hard to sit down and watch TV. I had to go outside and walk around the garden. I couldn't really relax. I was almost feeling success and extreme stress; a high and low at the same time.

It's very interesting. People say, "If I won the lottery, I would buy this and I would do this." But when you achieve it, you have to be prepared to handle it.

Because I'd worked so hard that when I achieved everything, it was very hard for me to kick in, because I'd worked so hard and so long for it.

Stanley: So how were you able to overcome your stress?

Andrew: Just recognizing that there is a time period when you have to work hard and pursue it, but there is a time when you have to relax as well. It's character building. Making money is only one thing. You've got to learn how to look after your money and manage it. You've got to learn how to spend time relaxing and spend time working. It's just time to break down your life into different segments where you can go and relax: sometimes you can go and work; sometimes you can go out and sort of party and have fun.

So it's just breaking down your life into different sections and understanding that this section is when I want to sit down and read a book for myself, this section is when I want to spend on my girlfriend. It's just breaking your life into different parts.

Stanley: What do you think are the three main ingredients to success as an Internet marketer?

Andrew: Three main ingredients? That is a good question.

1. **Determination.** You need to have determination and accept that you are going to fail many times. In fact, you're probably going to fail 99 times out of 100, but it's that one successful time that can do it.

2. **Understand why you are making money and where it's coming from.** When you start to experience a bit of success, you need to understand why you are making money and where it's coming from, and how to learn about gearing it up. How do you take it on to the next level? Don't try making money off one thing and then just try to move onto the next thing. Just stick with it and do it.

3. **To accept that you always have to invest in your education.** Any successful marketer, anybody who does well – like Mike Filsaime, Yanik Silver, John Reese, Russell Brunson etc – reads successful books. They know that they don't have all the knowledge and they're always looking to expand their knowledge and learn new things. You always have to be into learning new things.

The Internet is different to anything like radio or TV. It moves so fast, and you always need to keep yourself up to date. Some people, it's just too much of a fast-paced environment. Before, email marketing is good, but now there's pay-per-click advertising, there's video. It moves so fast that you need to understand that it's a fast-paced environment that you need to keep up with it.

Stanley: Absolutely. If you had a chance to change something about your present daily life, what would it be?

Andrew: At the moment, I'd just say at the moment, I'm quite happy. I wouldn't actually change things, because you can look back sometimes and see where you made a wrong decision. But it's all a learning curve, and any successful entrepreneur will always make mistakes.

The most important thing is you learn from your mistakes. As you stay in business longer, you become a bit wiser and you understand things a bit better. You understand that there are high points and low points, so you've just got to be prepared for that.

FINAL THOUGHTS

– *"You need to pick a mentor"*

Stanley: Name me one hero or role model who has influenced your life the most.

Andrew: Well, I probably have a few role models at different levels. I'm a very big admirer of Richard Branson of Virgin. I've read his book, *Losing My Virginity*, three times and I would recommend it to anyone. He started from scratch and built a multi-billion dollar empire.

But I also respect a lot of other people, like John Reese and the work he's done. And people like Yanik Silver, who is a very good friend of mine. He's a friend and mentor who has achieved a lot of success. If they need help or anything, I'm always there to help them, because of the help they've given me in the past. There is no limit to the amount of gratitude I have.

Having a mentor and someone to learn from is definitely very important. Going back to the three main ingredients, you need to pick a mentor, be it myself, Mike Filsaime, Yanik Silver. Pick someone and stick with them and become part of their family effectively.

Stanley: Andrew, I want to thank you for your time. Are there any final comments you want to add?

Andrew: Thanks very much for conducting this interview. You joined my coaching club and that's how we developed this relationship. It just goes to show the power of joining different coaching clubs and getting to personally know the people who are successful online in a particular element. I hope this information helps a lot of people out there, with mindset and focus, and how to start their own business.

Stanley: Do you want to let people know about your website?

Andrew: Yeah, sure. My coaching site is www.TheCBFormula.com, if anybody wants to come along and see it.

ABOUT THE AUTHOR

Stanley Tang is a 15 year-old Internet entrepreneur, author, and student from Hong Kong with a burning desire to succeed.

Ever since he began online in 2001, he has created numerous websites, launched multiple successful products, and generated tens of thousands of dollars on the Internet.

Having been on his own journey of discovery, Stanley brought together the world's top Internet millionaires to bring forth their behind-the-scenes stories of how they overcame adversities and rose to the top. And through his vision, share it with the world and inspire others to succeed and take action.

Visit his Internet marketing blog at http://www.StanleyTang.com.

CLAIM YOUR FREE BONUS IMMEDIATELY!

($397 VALUE)
HTTP://WWW.EMILLIONSBOOK.COM/BONUS

Thank you for your purchase of *eMillions!* As a reader of this book, you may now claim your free bonus gifts over at http://www.emillionsbook.com/bonus, including:

- Valuable audios
- Special reports
- Content-packed e-books
- Insider articles
- Exclusive videos
- Killer softwares
- Live teleseminars
- Premium site memberships
- And much, much more!

HTTP://WWW.EMILLIONSBOOK.COM/BONUS

Printed in the USA
CPSIA information can be obtained
at www.ICGtesting.com
JSHW012014140824
68134JS00025B/2420